A TOOLKIT FOR HAPPINESS

Things that make
human brains
HAPPY
hydration, nutrition, rest and sleep
positive social connections
living by your values, meaning + purpose
experiencing awe
music
Singing + dancing
moving your body
movement, exercise, stretching
Outside in nature
Blue + green spaces
play, fun and laughter
creativity and flow
Feeling valued
+ compassion
happy
dance

A TOOLKIT FOR HAPPINESS

55 WAYS TO FEEL BETTER

Dr Emma Hepburn
@thepsychologymum

greenfinch

Contents

The WELLBEING CURVE

adopted from Huppert 20[...]

We all move up + down the curve
& shift categories during our life

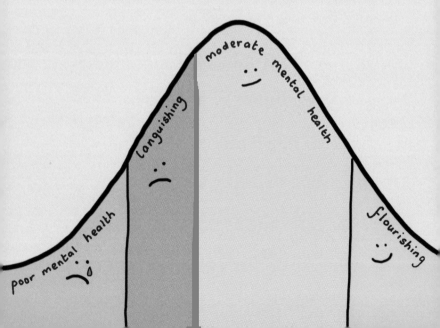

Introduction

I remember the exact moment when I read the Dalai Lama's words: 'I believe the purpose of life is to be happy' (in *The Art of Happiness*). As a 21-year-old searching for my purpose in life, these words stopped me in my tracks. Well, they stopped my first car in its tracks, because I was parked somewhere in the depths of Glasgow, next to a rusty lamppost, pondering over the gravity of these words, until I realized I was running late for my next home visit. The point of life was happiness itself. Simple. Yet, it blew my mind. Rather than something that came secondary to everything else, happiness was something I could work towards in itself. Was that rusty lamppost moment the turning point to a clinical psychology career that ultimately led to me working (in simplistic terms) to reduce sadness and improve happiness? I have no idea. Yet, here I am, over two decades later, writing a book about happiness with everything I've learned since I sat in my now defunct Ford Fiesta reading those words. I fully intend to go back to Glasgow and leave a copy of this book next to that same rusty lamppost to mark its publication.

I have to admit that writing a book about happiness in the middle of a global pandemic has had its challenges. To be truthful, some of the time when writing this book, I wasn't happy but was sad, worried and overwhelmed. It passed through my mind that perhaps I was somehow being hypocritical writing a book about happiness. Shouldn't I, a psychologist by trade and now a happiness author, remain a smiling beacon in the middle of whatever life was throwing at me?

Then I realized that I, or more accurately my brain, was buying into all those happiness myths we'll see in Chapter 1. I was telling myself that somehow I couldn't write about happiness without feeling perpetually happy, when, in fact, it's impossible to feel perpetually happy even at the best of times. Even worse, was I saying that somehow I had failed as a psychologist and happiness author by being sad? When, of course, suffering is an inevitable part of life and seeing happiness as successful or unhappiness as unsuccessful is, quite frankly, a doomed venture – and certainly not indicative of my ability as a psychologist or happiness author.

So it struck me that the reverse is true. It would be hugely hypocritical to pretend I am happy all of the time. Worse still, it would reinforce those happiness myths that continue to buzz around us, feeding into our beliefs, thoughts and behaviours. So, let's collectively shatter those myths. I'll start by being honest: I am not always happy. Not being happy or experiencing a range of different emotions simply makes me human. Perhaps in order to understand happiness fully, we also need to understand sadness, and all the other complex emotions that life throws at us. To me, happiness is as much about how we navigate these emotions as it is about building our lives towards happiness itself.

While I may not always be happy, I do have an advantage. Years of working with people to improve their wellbeing, researching and reading the evidence around happiness and sadness, and studying the functioning of the brain means that I am more likely to spot when my brain is working against me. I am well equipped to understand, respond to and shape my emotions. I know what to do to help when I feel bad, and I know, in theory, how to implement these actions (we'll come back to that a bit later, because it's not always easy to transfer theory to practice, even for a psychologist). What I hope this book will do is give you that same advantage – to help you build happiness into your life while also giving you a road map to navigate the inevitable bad times.

What the heck is happiness anyway?

If I asked 'Are you happy?', I'd guess you would answer by giving me an approximate summation of how you feel in and about your life, and lots of different factors would affect your response at different times. The summation of those elements in your life that come together to give you a sense of overall happiness. But what are those elements that can determine whether we are happy or not?

Positive momentary emotions

Let's start with experiences of momentary emotions by returning to that first question I asked: 'Are you happy?' You might have paused and thought, 'How do I feel right now?', and reflected on the specific emotion you were feeling in the moment. Having done a quick check and evaluated this, you might have told me 'yes' or 'no', and perhaps given me an alternative emotion instead – 'No, Emma, I am not feeling happy, in fact I am feeling…'

a) unease and a bit of dread that a complete stranger has asked me such a personal question.
b) confused, as I have just started reading this book, and as I'm only three pages in I don't know the magic happiness formula yet.
c) sad, as I've had a lot of difficult events over this last week.

I could go on, but I won't, as research suggests there are hundreds, even thousands, of different emotion words, so there are at least this number of possible answers to the question. When we think of happiness in these terms, we are thinking about particular emotions we are feeling at specific times. Emotions are transient and pass quickly, and we experience lots of emotions in any given day. So, if I was annoying and asked you this same question, say, 42 times in a day, I would most likely receive a huge range of answers.

These momentary emotions are important – people who report a greater overall sense of happiness also report greater overall experiences of positive emotions in their life, and vice versa. But momentary emotions are not the whole story. If they were, then surely it would be as easy as just increasing these nice, pleasant or positive feelings in life and reducing negative feelings. Nice and simple. Book done. Not quite, because there are some catches. Not all feel-good emotions make us feel good in the longer term. Feeling good all the time can sometimes feel meaningless. Our brain catches us out by not letting us feel good, or making us think we will feel good by doing certain things, when in fact we won't. Some of the ways we try to reduce negative feelings can reduce how good we feel. But the biggest catch is that just increasing daily positive emotions doesn't seem to be enough to contribute to that overall sense of happiness. So more positive emotions and less difficult emotions are a start. However, it seems as humans we need something more – and that something is meaning.

Meaning and purpose

It's not a new discovery that humans need meaning in life to be happy. Since the nature of happiness was first debated, meaning has been central to the argument. The Greek philosopher Aristotle thought happiness was a central purpose of human life – in fact, he would argue it's the ultimate purpose of human existence. When Greek philosophers discussed the nature of a life well lived, they talked about two concepts: hedonia and eudaimonia (yes, I had to google how to say that, too). To explain hedonia, think about hedonism – pleasure seeking, which is about the moment-to-moment emotions or feel-good sensations. Eudaimonia, on the other hand, is about a life well lived, and is akin to meaning and purpose in life – thought to be a less transient and more stable form of happiness.

This is all backed up by modern research, which confirms that experiencing meaning in life is associated with increased positive feelings, happiness and wellbeing, and is even linked to living a longer, healthier life. So, happiness may be the meaning and purpose of life, but it turns out meaning and purpose may also be the happiness of life.

Moving beyond happiness

I, however, am not a happyologist, I am a psychologist. This means talking about happiness alone is too narrow a concept. We need to broaden what we mean when I asked, 'Are you happy?' What does it mean to feel you have an overall sense of happiness? What makes you a well being? And therein lies a possible answer. Wellbeing may be a better concept to capture this overall sense of happiness. More specifically, flourishing or thriving means we feel we are doing well in life. Rather, the question might be, 'How are you doing in life?'

This captures the broader sense of happiness as doing well or feeling good overall. Again, there are multiple ways that wellbeing has and can be defined. According to the What Works Centre for Wellbeing (the organization used to measure wellbeing by the Office for National Statistics in the UK), the definition of personal wellbeing combines all the elements of happiness we've spoken about into an overarching concept and includes how satisfied we are with life, whether we believe that what we do in life is worthwhile, our day-to-day emotional experiences and our wider mental wellbeing. It is intrinsically linked to how we feel, and, therefore, our mental health. We can think of wellbeing as being on a continuum from poor wellbeing (possibly mental illness) to excellent wellbeing (often defined as flourishing or thriving) – as demonstrated in the illustration on page 4.

When I talk about happiness in this book, I mean that overall sense that we are doing well in life, that we are flourishing, that summation answer we give to the question, 'Are you happy?' I sometimes use the words 'happiness' and 'wellbeing' interchangeably to capture this concept.

The happiness sandwich

There are many happiness models out there, but I wanted one to represent the elements that contribute to happiness and how we can build it into life. My initial thought was a house but something about a happiness house bugged me. Unlike a house, building happiness needs to be a daily part of life, something we continuously build, that sometimes doesn't work well because other factors are impacting on it. I needed something that we build in everyday life to represent this. Then, one day, while making lunch for my two children, it came to me. A sandwich!

The happiness sandwich model isn't one that you will come across in psychology textbooks but it has all the elements I need. It's something we build regularly, it has a changeable and sometimes flimsy base, fillings we can add that depend on context and personal taste, and it requires tools (well, utensils) to build it. Finally, the amount of attention we give it and how we use it will affect how beneficial it is to us. So, readers, baguettes and bloomers, cheese or ham: here I present to you the happiness sandwich. I hope you can use this analogy to help build happiness in your life. We'll look more at the sandwich elements in Chapter 1, but for now it is a blank template, ready to be adapted as you learn what does and doesn't work for you, and which tools you need to build it as effectively as possible.

My happiness sandwich

How to use my attention for happiness:

tools that will help me build it

my beliefs + what I can do when they are unhelpful:

My meaning and purpose fillers:

what I can do in my context:

my positive emotion fillers:

ways to create a secure base:

how to build this into my daily life:

false fillers to chuck out

Happiness is..........

FACT

feeling lots of different emotions

only ever temporary

a skill that can be learned

something we often have to work on

something we can start building in the here + now

FICTION

always feeling happy

a place we arrive at

selfish

something you are born with, or not

something we have to wait for

never feeling sad or other difficult emotions

Chapter 1
Understanding Happiness

During my teenage years, if I browsed in any poster shop, I would have been guaranteed to flick past numerous posters with the slogan 'Happiness is…' This phrase would be followed by a host of sunsets, pretty pictures and funny captions about the meaning of happiness. Although seemingly trivial, these messages influence our beliefs about happiness and therefore what we think makes us happy and how we try to be happy. And it's not just 1990s posters that provide messages about the secrets of happiness – these messages are rife in media, adverts, among family, and in peer and society behaviour and beliefs, and they transmit into our brain to influence our thoughts on happiness. False messages lead to behaviours that we hope will result in happiness, but often take us down a different road. To build a robust happiness sandwich, we first need to understand when and why this happens. This chapter looks at separating the fact from the fiction of happiness, and understanding how the brain helps and hinders us to build a solid and effective happiness sandwich.

SMILE
you've reached
Happyland!
happiness is not a final destination
it is just somewhere you visit on the path of lif

Six myths of happiness

We started the book by looking at what happiness is, now it's time to think about what it isn't. Our beliefs about happiness can affect the choices we make, our thoughts and behaviours, and our happiness. We may add seemingly tempting ingredients to our happiness sandwich, in the false hope that they will make us feel better, but actually they leave us unfulfilled, wanting more or with a sour taste in our mouth. Knowing what happiness *isn't* can help us identify when we are adding false ingredients into the mix or have unrealistic expectations, and can enable us to make informed choices about what we do want to include or leave out.

Happiness myths abound in the messages we receive from society – in adverts, in media, and in the stories we are told, both overtly and covertly. Spotting these myths can help you think about how they impact on the ingredients of your happiness sandwich.

1. Happy ever after

When I used to read fairy tales to my daughter, I annoyed her by changing the 'happy ever afters' to 'they lived happily ever after until two years later when they started bickering and fighting, but in between they had lots of nice times too'. I'm not sure I was consciously aware of it, but I was attempting to dispel the myth that getting that partner, marriage, job, children…or whatever you are hoping for, will bring lasting happiness. This is known as the 'arrival fallacy' and it goes something like this: 'I'll be happy when…I get married/get that job/reach my ideal size/get that rainbow unicorn' – delete or add, as appropriate. It's not necessarily that these things won't contribute to your happiness, as they might (especially the rainbow unicorn); it's more that they probably won't have as much impact as you hope they will. Thinking about happiness in this way also means we are waiting for happiness to arrive in the future, which can stop us doing the things that help us feel better in the here and now. Even worse, some of the things we spend all our time working towards might not make us happy once we reach our destination. In short, focusing our limited time and energy working towards an unrealistic end goal is doomed to fail.

2. Destination Happyland

Happyland – a place where all your dreams come true. It's out there, you just need to find it. Surely that's the point of existence – to find our happy place where we are untouched by the ravages and stresses of life? Now, I would love to sell you tickets to Happyland but it wouldn't take long for the complaints to start flooding in about the unacceptable feeling of sadness, the stressors and strains that infiltrated the border, and the impermanent nature of happiness. Sadly, Happyland would go out of business quickly. What's so wrong with the notion of Happyland? Well, for a start, it's hugely unrealistic. Dan Gilbert, a Harvard Psychology Professor, tells us that, 'Happiness is not a destination, it's just somewhere you visit along the path of life.' Having this belief, knowing it won't last, can help us notice and appreciate the happy visits all the more. It's the very temporal nature of the emotion that lets us know we are happy, and it's the contrast to other states that makes it feel good. We may not enjoy 'negative' emotions, but if we realize they are a normal part of life, we aren't disappointed by them. We have realistic expectations and learn to live with only visiting Happyland, in the knowledge we will find more pockets of happiness in the future.

3. Maybe she's/he's/they're born with it…
Some people seem to find joy everywhere. So, if we don't, can we learn to be happy? If you see happiness as an intrinsic characteristic, you may start to think it's pointless even trying to be happy, as you 'just aren't that sort of person'. While there's no doubt your outlook affects how you approach and interact with the world, personalities are not static and can change with age and context.

Aristotle thought that happiness was a skill to learn rather than a trait, and modern research also tells us that happiness is better thought of in this way. Our childhoods lay down the foundation of our belief systems and how we interact with the world. However, the brain is designed to learn, so by understanding *how* we have developed patterns of thought and behaviours, we can then learn to create new ones. This is the basis for all psychological treatment, and there's strong evidence to say it works to improve our mood when we feel bad. There's also evidence that positive psychology techniques can push us further up the wellbeing curve, indicating that we can actually learn the skill of being happy.

4. Happiness is...never feeling sad or bad

It's an unfortunate thing that emotions are often divided into negative and positive categories. This can lead to a belief that we need only positive emotions. Yes, happiness is partly about feeling good more often and bad less often, but it's not about *not* feeling bad. First of all, let's think about these categories. Angry and sad are surely negative emotions? Yet sometimes anger has been my best ally when it's directed me to things which rightly aggrieve me and that I need to tackle. As for sadness, sometimes life can be sad, and it's important to recognize and validate this. Let's think of happiness, which is surely a positive emotion? I remember a time in my life when each new item I bought gave me pleasure in the short term, yet the debt it built up didn't make me happy at all. On the other hand, things that make us feel rubbish straight away (in my case exercise) make us feel good longer term. So negative emotions aren't always bad, and positive emotions don't always make us happy.

If we think we shouldn't feel bad, then when we inevitably do, we can feel we have done something wrong or criticize ourselves – which will make us feel worse. Suppressing negative emotions is taxing for your brain and body, and the resulting stress is likely to make you less happy. Improving how you feel is about understanding your emotions and responding helpfully, rather than getting rid of them.

5. Just choose happiness

Wouldn't it be wonderful if we could get out of bed every morning, say 'I choose happiness!' and feel like we are floating on clouds all day, carefree, basking in the sunshine. Yet, regardless of our choice, the clouds rain us down to earth to land in a big muddy puddle, leaving us feeling sad, soggy and fed up. Because, of course, it's not as simple as choosing happiness. If it were, I would have been out of a job a long time ago. There's also an insidious implication behind this concept. If we are able to choose happiness, then have we chosen unhappiness? This places the blame for unhappiness directly at the feet of people who are unhappy. This is not only deeply unhelpful for people who are depressed, but also fails to take into account the complex life histories, cultural, environmental and systemic factors, belief systems, brain mechanisms and behavioural patterns that contribute to how we feel. In my many years of working with people, I have met many people who struggle to know how to change the complex factors that make them feel bad, or who are in difficult situations that would make anybody feel bad. But have they chosen this? In one word: NO.

Each of us, even a psychologist who knows a lot about happiness theory, has a brain that is prone to the usual biases and belief systems, which influence how we feel. But, we can learn to notice how our brains, thoughts and behaviours sometimes don't help us, and we can manage them better and find ways to improve our wellbeing. So, we can't *choose* happiness, but we can choose to understand what influences our happiness and try to do the things in our daily lives that make us feel better.

6. Happiness is selfish

We may think that happiness is self-indulgent, or that factors that bring us happiness are; and so, we exclude them from our lives. Yet, being happier has a positive impact on the people closest to you as well as your wider social relationships. Studies suggest that improved wellbeing gives us more capacity to look after others, and can even increase patience and understanding. Happiness and compassion (to both yourself and others) are intrinsically linked. So, we could conclude that happiness is anything but selfish.

My personal beliefs about happiness

Use the following statements to try to examine your beliefs about happiness and if they are realistic or not.

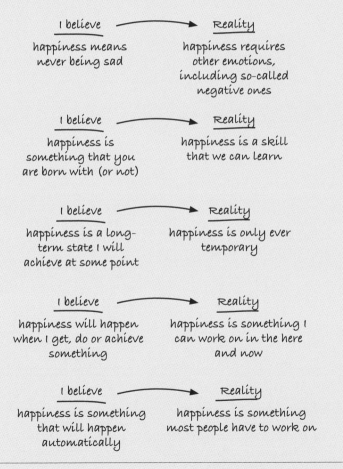

I believe ➝ Reality

happiness means never being sad

happiness requires other emotions, including so-called negative ones

I believe ➝ Reality

happiness is something that you are born with (or not)

happiness is a skill that we can learn

I believe ➝ Reality

happiness is a long-term state I will achieve at some point

happiness is only ever temporary

I believe ➝ Reality

happiness will happen when I get, do or achieve something

happiness is something I can work on in the here and now

I believe ➝ Reality

happiness is something that will happen automatically

happiness is something most people have to work on

your brain....

also your brain....

Happiness and the brain

Your brain is fundamental to being happy – it helps you feel and interpret emotions and evaluate your life. However, if you try to pinpoint what exactly it is in the brain that makes you happy, you might be searching for a while. There is no 'happy cortex'. To make it more complex, emotions are our interpretation of how we feel in our body – so perhaps this means that happiness is based in our body too? And, of course, the environment we live in is important for how we feel. So, happiness is also about context, and our senses and attention are the conduits to let that context into our brain, while our belief systems can be thought of as the filter that impacts on how we experience and evaluate our context.

Brains are wonderful, yet they can be downright unhelpful, especially when it comes to achieving happiness. In fact, I think you need to have some strong words with your brain regarding this goal, because despite the fact that most people will tell you the point of life is to be happy, your brain is probably going to disagree and tell you the point of life is to keep you safe and to process large amounts of information quickly, to make sure it can do just that. If your brain had a theme song, then the best fit would surely be Gloria Gaynor's 'I Will Survive'.

Imagine this argument between you and your brain.

In this scenario, while you might disagree, your brain would say it's doing its job. Ultimately, it's designed to spot threats and predict the future to help us survive. Sometimes this works well. For example, social connections keep us safe and help our species thrive, so our brain seeks them out. Good job, brain. Sometimes, it doesn't work so well. For instance, someone made one not-so-nice comment – your brain focuses on this and forgets all the nice parts of the day. Not such a good job, brain. What can we do about this?

Well, we need to appreciate that the brain is just doing what it is supposed to do. We can learn to spot and counteract these brain biases, or shortcuts, which enable us to process information quickly and survive but might not help make us happy. Let's look at some of these:

Shortcut 1: **Bad is stronger than good**

This is the name of a great psychology paper (see Further Reading, page 188) that summarizes all the ways the brain is more sensitive to bad information than good. The brain appears to have an inbuilt negative bias, which means it is vigilant for threat and is more likely to detect this in the environment. Throw some of life's bad experiences into the mix, and the brain is going to use its knowledge to predict future risks. For example, if you once spilt a pan of hot water on yourself, your brain will predict pans are a risk and increase its threat mode when it sees a full pan again. If nothing bad happens each time you see a full pan, gradually the brain will lower its prediction of risk. But this takes time, as the physiological impact of bad things last longer than the impact of good stuff. It appears we are doomed to remember the bad: we notice it more, our brain responds more intensely to it, we have stronger memories of it. It may seem as if the brain works against us when it comes to happiness. Why is this? To answer this, I return to your brain as Gloria Gaynor: *I will survive* – by spotting the bad, it learns to survive next time it happens.

Shortcut 2: **You get used to the good stuff**

When we notice the good, the brain tends to get used to it. So, what felt great at first, no longer feels so after a short time. This process is called 'hedonic adaptation'. Overall, this is thought to be helpful, and is sometimes described as a psychological immune system that helps us adapt to whatever life throws at us. If we stayed in heightened states for a long time it wouldn't be beneficial to us, so as humans we adapt to both good and bad. There are two ways in which we do this. The first is that the initial emotions reduce as time goes on and as life throws other stuff at us. Secondly, we start to take for granted circumstances or things that used to produce happiness. While this is also true of bad things, annoyingly we seem to adapt to good things much quicker. Negative bias means that good and bad things don't have equal impact on our lives. For example, after one bad day, people report reduced happiness but after one good day, people don't report increased happiness.

Shortcut 3: **Predicting how we will feel in the future**

The human brain has a wonderful ability to imagine the future. As Dan Gilbert puts it, 'Our brains were made for nexting and that's just what they'll do.' Yet anybody who has read science fiction novels from the mid-20th century will know that we are not very good at predicting the future. When we picture the future, we don't just think about what will happen, we anticipate how we will feel. This is called 'affect forecasting'. It enables us to plan for the future, makes us feel in control and, importantly, influences our decision-making in the here and now. Yet, here's the bad news: we're not that great at affect forecasting. We make incorrect predictions about the future and what will make us happy.

There are several brain biases at play here. We overestimate the impact that events will have on our life and how long this will last for. We think bad things will be worse and make us feel bad for longer than they actually do. There are a few reasons for this. When we imagine the future, we imagine one instance, not all the different possibilities that might happen. We also focus solely on the bad thing and forget all the other things in life that will also be going on. And vice versa for good things. So, when you imagine winning the lottery, you think about the nice house you will buy and the feeling you will get when you find out. You don't imagine having to deal with friends or relatives asking for money or feeling alienated from your peer group.

Emotions have a role to play here. The brain anchors itself in the present, which means it uses how it feels currently to create a projection bias – useful if you are feeling great, as you will be optimistic about the future. Not so great if you are feeling bad, as you will predict things won't be good. So, working with the brain is about noticing the predictions it is making and evaluating how helpful these are.

Working with your brain

So, what are we going to do with you, brain? We may not be able to override the way the brain works, but understanding it can help us recognize when our brain is hindering our happiness and work out what to do. We'll discover over the course of this book more ways to respond to negative bias and help your brain spot, observe and savour the good. This exercise is designed to help you spot when these brain shortcuts are at work and start to think about simple ways you can respond.

HELPFUL WAYS
TO RESPOND

EXAMPLES OF
NEGATIVE BIAS

Despite getting lots of positive feedback, you are devastated by one (sort of) negative comment.

Consider what went well. Mull this over to help your brain remember it.

Mulling over your day, your brain immediately thinks about the difficult or negative parts.

Try to widen your brain's focus to see positive aspects too. For example, if you had one negative comment about your work, balance this by counting how many positive comments you received. Focus on these to override your brain's attraction to the bad.

EXAMPLES OF ADAPTATION TO POSITIVE EVENTS

HELPFUL WAYS TO RESPOND

Positive events seem to have little impact on your life and you skip on to the next thing, barely noticing they have happened.

Notice the good things. Reflect on tasks you have done well today, what made you happy and/or proud? The more you focus on these, the more you remember them, and the longer-lasting the effects on your brain and emotions.

Don't wait for big things – celebrate the everyday small achievements.

Find ways to help you remember, such as taking pictures and talking things through.

EXAMPLES OF AFFECT FORECASTING

HELPFUL WAYS TO RESPOND

You cancel events because you are feeling gloomy, so predict you will not enjoy them (when history tells us you would).

Test it out with an experiment. How much do you think you will enjoy it, from 1–10, and how much did you actually enjoy it? Check if your predictions about how you would feel were correct. Write this evidence down, for next time. This is a better predictor of how you will feel than your thoughts.

You feel anxious about a forthcoming event so think it will be terrible. Once you go, you find it's not as bad as you thought and you start to enjoy yourself.

Five barriers to happiness

Happiness is ultimately about the day-to-day decisions and actions we take in life, and to increase our wellbeing, these need to be consistent with things that impact positively on our lives. We've seen that our beliefs about happiness are important, as they shape our predictions, decisions and actions. Due to hedonic adaptation or unrealistic expectations, many of the places we expect to find happiness just don't deliver. So, what influences our beliefs about happiness? Our family stories as we grow up, societal messages we are given explicitly and implicitly, and our experiences. Our brain builds its belief systems based on what it's been told, and what it's experienced so far.

One of the things that always strikes me when I read research on wellbeing is how often societal messages about what we should do are in direct contrast to what the studies tell us make us happy. Society says – get more things, make more money, get promoted, be busy, always be happy, achieve more and never, ever fail. Now you've done all that, strive for more. Yet, the irony is that striving for these things usually doesn't make us happy, and actually achieving these things almost never makes us happy. But those societal beliefs drive our decisions, behaviours and beliefs. That's why we often look for happiness in all the wrong places. We need to take these societal beliefs to task and question why we fall for them hook, line and sinker. Let's look at some of these beliefs and barriers in more detail.

1. Striving narrative

You'll have spotted a common thread in what society tells us: strive for more, seek betterment, do more, be more, look for self-fulfilment and self-improvement. This gets us on what's called the hedonic treadmill. When we strive, we search constantly for the next thing, or how to better ourselves, believing we are not enough just as we are. We also think that we won't be happy unless we reach these places, have money or fame, or whatever. Yet, research shows that achieving these goals often doesn't bring the happiness we desire (think back to hedonic adaptation), and so we end up tied to the hedonic treadmill, constantly running towards the next thing and never pausing to appreciate what we *do* have and what we have achieved. We are too distracted to pay attention to what we already can do in our lives, which can add to our wellbeing now. We are constantly reaching for the next goal and forget to think about the here and now. That's not to say achievement doesn't make our goal-orientated brains feel good – I love it when I achieve certain tasks. However, if we think that happiness lies solely in future achievement rather than in the process of working towards it, then it can serve to make us unhappy.

2. Immediate reward vs long-term happiness

The brain's reward system is an important part in feeling pleasure and is linked closely to learning and memory. This makes sense – if we remember the things that make us feel good, we will hopefully seek them again in the future (think food, social connections, sex). The brain's reward system gets excited about anticipating the reward, possibly even more than receiving it. While this often helps us, sometimes it works against us, as the things that make us feel great pleasure in the short term don't always make us feel very good in the longer term. Yet the brain's reward system is drawn powerfully towards them and we can start to believe we need the short-term rewards we crave in order to make us happy, when, in fact, they don't bring happiness.

The most obvious examples of this are drugs and alcohol. People use them because they make them feel good in the short term – they chemically activate the reward system, so we crave them. But in the long term, they can be detrimental to our happiness. Social media is another good example. As humans, we like gaining approval, so 'likes' inevitably make us feel good. Yet, if we load too much meaning on them or feel bad when we don't get them, our reward system has started to work against us. Even worse, when they make us feel bad in the long run, we sometimes start to seek that immediate reward even more, creating an unhelpful cycle. So, we need to notice when this happens. Now that sounds nice and easy, doesn't it? But the pull of the reward system is strong, and even though we know rationally that something is ultimately bad for us, our reward system draws us in.

3. Permitting happiness

Another narrative that influences our behaviour negatively is the belief that we shouldn't allow ourselves happiness. This can be tied to productivity – we believe we should be working and achieving to prove our worth. We therefore feel bad when we are doing something that we enjoy, because we believe we should be doing something more productive. Things that bring us happiness become secondary acts, only permissible when we have achieved everything else.

There are lots of other ways we don't permit ourselves to feel good. We may be scared it will end or we will jinx a happy moment if we let ourselves enjoy it. Or we may have negative beliefs about experiencing positive emotions, for example, 'I shouldn't feel pride as it's gloating'. Our beliefs about ourselves can get in the way if we don't think we deserve to feel happy. However, incorporating positive emotions and experiences into life should not be an afterthought. These activities, and the feel-good emotions they create, are beneficial for your brain, body, health and happiness level. Research suggests that they may even help you live longer. They are the very fabric of life and need to be seen as central to happiness.

4. Desperately seeking happiness

What happens when happiness itself becomes part of the striving narrative? When we view happiness as something we have to constantly pursue? Research suggests if we try too hard to be happy, then this can be detrimental. 'Woah, hold on a minute!', you might say. 'If that's the case, then why am I reading this book?' Well, let's get back to expectations. If you are reading this book in the hope that it will provide the magic formula that will make you perpetually happy, then alas you'll be disappointed, as we already know that's not realistic.

If we view happiness as the ultimate end goal, we can feel we have failed if we don't reach it, which leads to more unhappiness. And, of course, we are never going to reach this nirvana, as Happyland doesn't exist. But don't return the book just yet. Happiness is not an ultimate end goal or specific emotion to strive for, it is a process. Our aims are to understand ourselves, our emotions and our wellbeing (and what contributes to these). By doing so, we can learn to live our day-to-day life in line with what is meaningful to us, contributes positively to our wellbeing and in a way that works well for us.

5. Disregarding the importance of context

They say money can't buy happiness, and to a certain extent, that is true. However, what is strikingly true is that not having enough money causes unhappiness. Poverty is stressful and can impact on wellbeing through multiple mechanisms. Context can impact on wellbeing in many other ways. If we do not feel safe, if our world is vastly out of control, if we can't meet our basic needs, then this will impact on our health and happiness. That's not to say you can't have happy moments, but for overall health and happiness we need to feel a level of safety and security and be able to meet our basic needs. That is why we can't only look at happiness on an individual level, as we often tend to do in Western society. We need to look at the context for happiness on a community and society level, so we give people the means to achieve happiness and wellbeing. If you feel unhappy in difficult circumstances, you are not doing anything wrong.

It's important to acknowledge that everything I speak about in this book may not be beneficial if your situation is the main barrier to happiness. If the contextual building blocks for happiness aren't in place, and your base isn't safe and secure, then that base will need to be built before delving into the finer details.

Use the illustration in the exercise opposite to identify your own happiness barriers and what might help you to deal with them.

Identifying barriers to happiness

the happiness sandwich
Attention
tools to
help you build it
beliefs
I believe
what am I doing here?
false fillings
I'm a big dollop of meaning
meaning & purpose
INPUT
and I feel good
positive emotions
your base
I wannabe strong & secure
CONTEXT
OUTPUT

Understanding your own happiness

This section gives you a model that you can build on as you go through the book, but also as you go through life. There is no simple happiness formula, and what works in your happiness sandwich will be down to your personal tastes and preferences – which will be as varied as real sandwich filling preferences (cheese and Pringles, anyone? No? Just me then). It's about thinking, noticing and understanding what works for you (which may change as life changes), and realizing when that pesky brain of yours is working against you. Paying attention to what makes you feel good is a learning process. It allows you to make conscious decisions with the aim of building your own happiness sandwich as effectively as you can, thinking about how you can use it and monitoring if it is still working for you. The happiness sandwich is not just about making you happy, it is also about understanding the factors contributing to how you are feeling and what you can do about these when they occur.

Use the exercises on the following pages to identify what should be included in your happiness sandwich. Fill in the template on page 15 and, as you read through the book, add in how you can ensure your attention, beliefs, context and what you do with your sandwich can help improve happiness.

How happy are you?

Let's start with an idea of where your happiness levels are right now by using the scale below. Remember, this is not about always feeling happy (impossible) but about understanding how you are feeling and where (if possible) you can target your actions.

Where is your current happiness level?
What made you choose this level?
What is impacting on how you feel?
What needs to happen to improve this?

Building your happiness sandwich

Once you've worked out your happiness from the scale, you can start to think about building your sandwich. Use the illustration on page 42 to think about what you will put in your sandwich and add these to your own happiness sandwich template on page 15.

Step 1: Sandwich bun – bottom layer (the base for happiness)
Without a base, you can't add any of the happiness fillings. Is this base missing altogether? It is important to think about whether there are any factors in your life that are consistently detrimental to your happiness by making you feel unsafe, frequently stressed or lacking in energy. These will limit how many fillings you can put in. Is there anything that can be tackled? Is there anything you need help to tackle?

Basic self-care, managing stress, improving sleep, diet and hydration are all factors that help strengthen your base and enable you to do things that you know improve your wellbeing (the sandwich fillings). These provide the energy and building blocks that our brain and body require to enable us to feel good physically. Without them, our sandwich base may not be able to hold its filling adequately.

Step 2: Sandwich bun – top layer (the container of happiness)
This layer represents our beliefs. Beliefs can help construct the sandwich or be detrimental so that it gives way at the first bite, with all the ingredients splootering (as we say in Scotland) down your sweater. For example, your beliefs might say that working all

the time will make you happy, so you continue adding long work hours as a mistaken ingredient. Your beliefs about happiness are also important. If you don't think your sandwich is of value, then you are probably going to leave it languishing in a bag, only to be discovered a bit mouldy in a few weeks' time. If you think you don't deserve to be happy, then you'll ignore the sandwich.

Here, think about your beliefs on happiness and which of these are helpful to you – which help to construct a nice, easy-to-hold sandwich? Which are unhelpful and will make the sandwich give way when you bite into it? Identifying your beliefs isn't always easy, and changing them can be even harder, but starting to think about them so that you can identify barriers to happiness can be helpful. Use the exercises earlier in this chapter (see page 41) to help with this. We'll also look at how other beliefs may get in the way of happiness later in the book (see pages 90–7).

Step 3: **Picking the sandwich fillers – middle layer**

Now that you've constructed your bun, you can start thinking about the ingredients that are going to fill your sandwich. Don't worry if you struggle with knowing what fillings to add. We'll continue to discuss factors that have been shown to improve wellbeing throughout the book, and you can add in more as you go through these sections.

• What makes you feel good (positive emotion fillers)?

Note down all the things that bring you joy, pleasure or other feel-good emotions. These can be things that make you feel good in the here and now or things that make you feel good after you've done them. Remember, though, we can be bad at predicting this correctly, so this list may need to be revised as time goes on, as we discover our projection of what will make us happy is not necessarily correct. For me, positive emotion fillers include seeing friends, playing with my children and enjoying good food (some of these also give me meaning and purpose – see below).

One way to help with this is to get a real-time measure of how your experiences make you feel, instead of basing your fillings on predictions. Try to rate how good you feel after an action or activity on a scale of 1 to 10 and describe the emotions you felt. Like anything though, remember that just doing something once is not enough to give you a representative sample. For example, the first time you do something you might hate it because you had a headache coming on; but the other times you try it, you may enjoy doing it. You will need to trial this over time for a fair view of how different activities make you feel and which you want to add into your sandwich.

• **What gives you a sense of meaning and purpose?**
Remember, happiness is not just about experiencing positive emotions – it's also about meaning and purpose. In order to taste right, the sandwich needs a balance between these ingredients. Think about what is meaningful to you. We know that living a life in line with your values and what is important to you improves wellbeing, so you can use a values exercise to think about this more (see Further Reading, pages 188–9). Think about the things you do that provide you with meaning and purpose. There can be overlap – what gives us pleasure may also provide meaning and purpose, and vice versa. For me, helping people at work gives me meaning and purpose – it can be hard but ultimately, it makes me feel good.

Step 4: Identifying mistaken ingredients

We don't always choose the right ingredients for our sandwich. Which sandwich fillers taste good initially but leave a sour taste in your mouth after a short time? Note these in this section.

• What turns out to be a short-term reward?

These are things that make us feel great only for one bite then leave a sour taste, so we realize we shouldn't have included them. This is not about regret or shame for enjoying ourselves, but rather about understanding the brain's reward system, which is built to chase and anticipate short-term rewards but not to bring a more long-lasting sense of wellbeing. Sometimes the short-term reward is detrimental to our happiness overall: for example, our phones draw us in with a short term burst of reward but end up distracting us from the things that make us feel good in real life.

• Which things did you expect to bring you happiness but didn't?

These are the false fillings in our sandwich that we come to realize we don't actually like and/or don't deliver what we thought they would. They might be based on societal messages or false expectations. For example, you may have believed being a certain weight or accruing a particular number of followers on social media would make you happy, but when you got there you realized it didn't make you any happier.

Step 5: Your sandwich exists in the world

There are a few other factors that impact on your sandwich fillings and how much you might enjoy them.

• Input

This can be thought of as your attention, which helps decide what goes into your sandwich. Attention interacts closely with your belief systems (your internal world and thoughts) and influences what you put into your sandwich. It can affect how much focus you give to improving your overall wellbeing and whether your fillers are beneficial – do you savour those fillings in your happiness sandwich or are you distracted by something else, for example looking at your phone, so you never notice the effects? Remember that attention is also affected by your brain shortcuts. The threats to your happiness will be spotted much more quickly than the things that would make you very happy if only you spotted them.

• Output

This can be thought of as how you continue to ensure you make your happiness sandwich meaningful and useful in your day-to-day life. Do you just build it once and then forget to use it? Or do you keep that sandwich updated, make sure you continue to change the filling when you need to, and remember to use it at the right points in your life? If our sandwich is built with sound knowledge, will we then use it consistently in a way that continues to benefit us?

• Context

Finally, we can never take the sandwich out of its context, or your environment. Context influences our happiness sandwich in a number of ways. It helps build, and continues to contribute to, our belief systems. Your context also influences what you are able to put in your sandwich and, importantly, it can destabilize it by weakening its base. For example, if you are surrounded by people who belittle you, it creates stress (which impacts on your base) and can also impact on your belief system.

Things that make human brains happy

hydration, nutrition, rest and sleep

positive social connections

living by your values, meaning + purpose

experiencing awe

moving your body

movement, exercise, stretching

Outside in nature

Blue + green spaces

play, fun and laughter

creativity and flow

Feeling valued

compassion

Music

Singing + dancing

happy dance

Chapter 2
What Makes Us Happy?

We've looked at some of the mistaken beliefs about happiness and its causes, and how these can drive us to work against ourselves. Hopefully this has helped you identify mistaken ingredients in your happiness sandwich, or factors in your life that are creating barriers to wellbeing. Now it's time to start thinking about which fillers we want to put in that will make us feel better. This chapter looks at what might make us feel good. Again, each topic doesn't contain exact prescriptive happiness tablets – life is a bit more complex than that. The topics are better thought of as categories from which you can choose the specific type of ingredients or range of things that works best for you to achieve these aims. Don't forget that happiness is a process, so you often need to test things out to see how they work in your life at that moment in time. Not all will work, and neither should they, as your life fillers need to be selected and tested personally to find the best combination to suit your circumstances, strengths and skills. Try things out for yourself, a few times and in different ways, even if it seems unusual or different at first, because you can only help your brain learn if it works for you (or not) by giving things a go.

Connecting for happiness

Whereas money, possessions and career success are not strong predictors of wellbeing, there's something which is a far stronger predictor of long-term happiness than anything else on Earth. In fact, it's so important that our brain is specifically designed to do it. So, what is this amazing thing? It's what you do when you share a silly cat meme, have a good old moan about your boss at work, or when you read your kids a bedtime story. Yes, it's social connections. The jury is unanimous when it comes to this one. Study after study shows that having positive social connection in our life improves how we feel, our mental and physical health, and even how long we live for. The evidence is so strong that Robert Waldinger, the lead researcher of the long-term Harvard Adult Development Study, which has been looking at wellbeing in students from Harvard University and their children for over 70 years, concluded that, 'The good life is good relationships.' That's a powerful conclusion.

The opposite of connection could be thought to be isolation. Research into loneliness (feeling and being alone not through choice) suggests this has the opposite effect on us as humans – we feel more stressed and have poorer health. This shows up in our body with increased physiological markers of stress, which are linked to poorer health and wellbeing.

Why are good quality social relationships so beneficial for us? There are lots of reasons. Sharing emotions and talking through things with someone else can help us to process information, reduce the stress we feel and impact positively on us. It can also help us see things in a different way, giving us extra brain space and sometimes even practical help to solve problems. Being with other people gives meaning and purpose to life. We are provided with opportunities to help and support others. We can talk about and share positive experiences, which prolongs the amount we think about and remember these experiences, which in turn helps extend the positive effect they have and reduces hedonic adaptation. Sharing also helps us deal with difficult emotions and can enhance joyful emotions (laughing is inherently good for us and seems to occur far more when with other people). Relationships enable us to do things, help us achieve goals, and being surrounded by people with similar values makes us feel safe and validated.

The old adage of quality rather than quantity is crucial here, because it's the quality of relationships, and how connected we feel, that is the important factor. For close relationships, it's about building trust, which makes us feel safe. Yet, we have to recognize that this doesn't come naturally to all of us. Depending on your experiences and resultant belief systems, it's sometimes a lot harder than it sounds to trust others.

Social connection can take different forms. Connecting with a group of people with similar interests or going through similar difficult experiences, helps normalize how you feel. Feeling you are somehow different is isolating, whereas seeing the shared nature of your experience is inherently validating. Even the small life connections – smiling as you pass someone, the knowing glance in a meeting as someone talks for too long – are important and can make us feel connected to those around us. Another way to look at the benefits of connection is thinking about social capital: the ability to obtain benefits from the pool of people around you, for example, sharing the school pick-up. While this might sound self-serving, the interconnectedness of social networks means that helping others confers mutual benefit to both parties, even more so to the person providing. So, being social adds to your resources, and helps you solve problems.

Connections don't have to be human. Feeling connected to animals provides both pleasure and purpose. Feeling connected to nature also provides benefits, which we'll look at more later. Thinking about how to make connections is important. However, this will mean different things to different people. Whatever other happiness fillings you choose, social connections should be a priority ingredient.

The following exercises look at specific ideas that have been shown to improve wellbeing.

Adding connections to your happiness sandwich

Connections are so crucial for happiness and wellbeing that they should be a standard part of any sandwich, in a way that works for you. Use these prompts to consider what connections mean to you, so you can add them into your happiness sandwich (see pages 45-9), along with the specific ideas in the other exercises.

- *When do I feel most connected?*

- *What helps me feel connected?*

- *How can I include these in my life?*

Kindness and helping

My daughter says she prefers spending her pocket money on others, and she's onto something, because acts of kindness boost wellbeing, increase positive emotions, reduce negative ones and build social connection, meaning and sense of purpose. Research shows little actions may be as, or even more, beneficial than big ones, with one article suggesting that five tiny things make us feel better than one bigger thing. Think about little acts of kindness you can fit into your day. Hold the door open, smile at someone, send photos of shared memories to friends or simply say thank you. There are lots of ideas on the Action for Happiness website if you need suggestions (see Further Reading, pages 188-9).

Building empathy

Being empathetic means thinking about what someone else might be feeling. We all have lots going on underneath the surface, and being empathetic recognizes this and tries to understand instead of judging what we see, which is only ever the tip of the iceberg. Happiness is linked to being able to empathize, as it can make us more patient and tolerant, lead to feeling connected, and we also benefit from sharing others' positive emotions. So next time you find yourself judging someone, pause and step back. Think about what you *can't* see – what's underneath the surface? Widening our understanding can make us think and behave towards the person differently. This simple illustration is designed to help you do this.

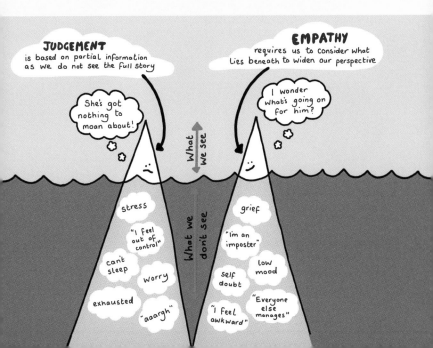

"Why" Planets
What's your meaning + purpose?

phoning parents

bedtime stories

family

family trips

game nights

I am a Why planet.
I am what gives you meaning
and purpose - your why

We are your Why moons-
the small daily things you do
that connect you to your why

over the
moon to
meet you

writing

cooking meals

creativity

reading

gardening

we are jus
some examp

finding
new
foods

planning events

learning

watching
nature
programmes

hearing
others'
perspective

fill us in with your
own Whys such as music
friends, helping etc.

Meaning, purpose and happiness

Humans naturally find meaning in things. The brain sifts through millions of data points and finds the patterns, so we can process information effectively. We find meaning in tones of voice and facial expressions, we work out perceptually the meaning of sensory data (that's a grey thing with a fuzzy tail eating nuts – that must mean it's a squirrel). We often puzzle over the meaning of something: what did she mean by the wording of that text? The meaning we give to something helps us understand it and consider how to respond. We are so inclined to make sense of everything that we also find meaning in random data when there is none – this is called 'apophenia', and we do it a lot – we find meaning when someone phones at the moment we are thinking of them, we look for 'signs' to help us make decisions, and look for meaning in the tea leaves in the bottom of the cup. Often this helps us make sense of difficult things (although sometimes the 'meaning' we find can be unhelpful, such as conspiracy theories). Meaning-making in its basic sense is fundamental in helping us make sense of things in our world, feel in control, understand and know how to respond.

The same applies to higher forms of meaning. As humans, we like to find purpose in our lives. Viktor Frankl, a psychiatrist who was imprisoned in a concentration camp in World War II, thought that the search for meaning was central to man's existence, and that our primary job was to discover it and build it into our life. Quoting philosopher Friedrich Nietzsche, Frankl wrote that, 'Those who have a "why" to live, can bear with almost any "how".' If we understand our meaning, then we have our 'why', which we can construct our lives around. Not only is meaning central to the concept of happiness itself, but research suggests it helps us cope with stressors, feel better, have improved health and possibly even brain functioning, and helps us live longer. Having meaning, therefore, appears to be a fundamental component of happiness, which is why it's a core filling in our sandwich.

Sometimes the same things give us both joy and meaning, such as reading to your kids or having a laugh with friends. That's not always the case, though. Research suggests having children, for example, doesn't do much for your day-to-day positive feelings (in fact, you often feel bad because of lack of sleep, stress and time famine), but people report that having a baby-sized dollop of purpose makes them happy. I think the same could be said about writing a book. While sometimes it feels fantastic and joyful, at other times it feels difficult and not very joyful at all. However, overall I am working towards something that gives me a purpose, and the thought that this might have even a tiny beneficial impact on someone else is extremely meaningful to me. So, finding meaning doesn't have to be all singing and dancing triumphant joy; sometimes pleasure and purpose seem to be quite distinct.

However, we need to find the right balance for our sandwich: too much meaningful activity that only brings positive feelings in the long term (this could be thought of as waiting for happiness) would most likely make our happiness sandwich taste bad in the short term, and is not enough for that overall sense of happiness. We also need positive emotions in the here and now, to make the sandwich tasty on the first bite *and* have a long-term beneficial effect.

What do we mean by 'meaning'? It's your 'why' – it's what makes your life feel worthwhile and gives you purpose. It's not some grandiose search for your life's ambition, it's about the small daily things that bring meaning to your life. Sometimes, it's as simple as focusing on why a task is meaningful to you, or thinking about how you can increase meaningful things in your life. Meaning is often understood in terms of values. These are the things that are important to you, a direction in life that you can build your goals around. Living life consistently with what is important to you has been shown to make you feel better. Understanding your meaning can help you decide which goals to pursue and which ingredients you put into your happiness sandwich.

What's your 'why'?

Using the illustration on page 58, identify daily tasks that give you meaning. You can work backwards or forwards from the moons (activities) to the planets (meaning) or vice versa. If you are not sure what gives you purpose, start by identifying your values – what is meaningful to you. Some examples of values could be helping people, creativity or sustainability. Next think about which activities fit with those values. There are many values exercises online which you can use (see Further Reading, pages 188-9). Another way is to think about the things you do that make you feel purposeful. Cluster these together to identify if there is an overarching theme (the planet) that unifies these daily things. Here are some questions to help you:

• *Stop and think about what you do on a daily basis. What do the tasks you have done today mean to you? Which tasks do you find meaningful or give you purpose? Why is this?*

• *What creates a spark in you? What do you do that makes you feel great or engaged? Are there themes to these?*

• *Pause and think about the meaningful ways you are connected. What do the connections you have mean to you?*

• *When you look back over your life so far, what has given you a sense of purpose?*

• *If you reflect on your life, what do you think would stand out as the most meaningful activities you have done? What would it look like to be acting on this meaning during a day, week or month?*

Ultimately, you want to think about how you can include activities (the moons) that give you meaning (the planets) in your life regularly and that you can include as your happiness fillings. Don't worry if this exercise is hard – it can be, and you may need to think about it for a while. Don't feel like a failure if you can't identify your planets quickly; let yourself mull over it, notice what gives meaning and purpose in your day and take your time.

Committing to something bigger

An important component of meaning is thought to be committing to something bigger than yourself. This shifts us beyond our individual goals to align with greater purpose, which can make us feel connected and confers all the benefits of community and helping others. For some people this might come naturally if they have religion, family or community in their life. But not always. Sometimes you may need to think about how you can do this. For example, if one of your values is the environment, could you commit some time to an environmental organization or do a local beach clean? If it's kindness, could you introduce an initiative at work or distribute kindness somehow in your community (e.g. donate to a food bank)? Use these questions to get you thinking:

• *What are my values? Are there any ways I can commit to these at a wider level? Family, community, society?*

• *What skills do I have? Can I share these in any way? How can I use these skills beyond myself?*

Experiencing awe

Awe is a big emotion but one that is often overlooked. Awe is about being amazed, surprised or feeling wonder. It's about seeing something bigger than yourself. It has been described as a positive emotion people experience when they are in the presence of something vast that they cannot immediately understand or fit with their existing knowledge base. When we feel awe, our focus shifts from our own internal world to the wider, external world, leading us to perceive ourselves as being less significant, or 'smaller', and also making us feel more connected to our life, community or world.

Children see awe everywhere. Think of those frustrating walks to the shop, which should have taken five minutes but took an hour because they were distracted by leaves, bugs, rocks and mud. But as our understanding grows, our sense of awe lessens and we are caught up more in our internal world. However, there's evidence emerging that you can cultivate a sense of awe, which is good for happiness and health. Here are some ways of cultivating awe that have shown positive results.

Awe walks: new places are most likely to elicit a sense of awe, so start with even a slightly different route to normal. Reduce distractions, don't take your phone and focus on the external environment. Try to notice things you have never seen, smelt, heard or felt before. Try to see the unexpected – what is unusual on your walk? Shift your focus from the tiny (e.g. plant structures, light patterns, bird calls) to the vast (e.g. the sky, the overall landscape, sounds). Notice how each of these things makes you feel. If you find yourself caught up in your internal world, focusing on thoughts or worries, don't berate yourself – take a few slow breaths and shift your focus back to aspects of the external world.

Short awe breaks: when feeling stressed, pausing to take a look at awe-inspiring landscapes, videos, images or sounds can induce positive feelings. Instead of reaching for your phone, consider taking an awe break. Perhaps a five-minute pause at the end of a task, or a regular two minutes throughout the day to look, listen or hear something that fills you with wonder. Listen to Martin Luther King's speech, watch a nature clip or an inspiring sporting feat (I go for Eddie the Eagle every time). I've put some ideas in the Further Reading section to get you started (see pages 188–9).

Awe-inducing experiences: awe is all around us. The most common awe-inducing experiences relate to the natural world and other people. Here are some ideas:

• *Notice changes in the natural environment, such as when the leaves start turning.*

• *If you have children, watch how they interact with the world and share in their sense of awe.*

• *Visit a museum or gallery and spend time looking and thinking about what you see.*

• *Take a 'photo walk', even just around the house: take photos of things you see that inspire you or make you feel awe and wonder.*

• *Look outwards at buildings, trees, clouds, the moon and stars.*

3 tiny things for happiness
one thing that.....
brings me joy
I look forward to
makes me laugh
makes me feel connected
relaxes me
nurtures me
gives me a sense of achievement
choose at least 3 tiny things to do daily

Enabling happiness

Feeling good is a fundamental part of happiness. We often describe these feelings as positive emotions, and that's because not only do they make us feel good, they also have a positive impact on our body and health. Feeling emotions such as joy, pleasure, pride and calm sets off a series of reactions in our brain and body that can manage stress, help us relax, help our body heal, our immune system work better and, ultimately, help us function better and live longer. So, these emotions are an extremely important part of our lives. Experiencing regular feel-good emotions is a fundamental part of happiness, which is why it's a crucial filler for our happiness sandwich.

However, all too often we don't place enough importance on these emotions. Of course, you can't feel good all the time, and many of the things in our lives have an important purpose (such as work to keep us financially sound) but might not always make us feel good. But, we do need to prioritize building the things that make us feel good into our lives as primary objectives, not just when your to-do list is done, or slotted in when possible. Feeling good should not be an afterthought, it should be an end in itself.

Let's come back to the barriers and myths about happiness, which can unintentionally make feeling good feel bad. We tell ourselves we should be working and we are slacking if we take a break. We feel lazy, unproductive and self-indulgent when sitting down to relax or taking time for ourselves. If we don't feel stressed, we aren't working hard enough. These beliefs are insidious for our happiness. We need to stand up to them and the negative impact they have on our lives. There is no stronger counter argument than this: doing things that make you feel good and create positive emotions are important for your mental and physical health. They are not secondary aims, but fundamental for you as a human to live your life well, connect with other people, function and feel happy. They are part of what it means to live life well.

Once you've successfully convinced yourself of the importance of feeling good, and including regular activities that make you feel this way, it's time to incorporate them into your life on a daily basis. While big things are important, it's the daily pockets of positive emotion that are likely to have the most beneficial impact on your health and happiness.

Seven ideas for daily positive emotion

Here are some ideas of activities that have been shown to consistently create positive emotion and that you could consider incorporating into your happiness sandwich.

1. Movement

Physically, movement sets off a chain of events in the body that contributes positively to how we feel. It releases brain chemicals that make us feel good, helps manage and reduce the stress response, allows our brain to grow and form new connections, and increases blood flow to our brain, which improves cognition and thinking. Add in the psychological benefits – a sense of achievement, often being outside, connecting with other people – and we can consider movement a big win for your happiness. Add in the long-term benefits of being physically fitter and we have an exponential win. The research agrees with me (or, more accurately, I agree with it). A wealth of studies suggest that exercise improves happiness and reduces depression and anxiety symptoms. So, movement is an essential ingredient of any happiness sandwich. How you add it in can take many forms, from walking, dancing, golf or even roller-skating – whatever floats your movement boat. Even very small bouts of exercise during your day, such as regularly getting up from your desk or getting out for short walks, can be effective to improve wellbeing.

2. Green space and blue space

If the Covid-19 pandemic has taught us anything, surely it's that there's something special about being in open space, in nature (green space) and near water (blue space). Access to green and blue space is related to positive moods and reduction in negative mood states and stress. Experiential studies indicate that people feel happiest when in these spaces. There may be lots of ways these types of spaces help our happiness. Perhaps there's something inherently relaxing about the environment itself, so we find them restorative. It may be because we are often moving, socially interacting or relaxing in some way in this space, which feeds into our happiness. Then there's the other factors such as fewer pollutants and traffic noise, and increased levels of light and vitamin D for our bodies. Whatever the reasons, getting outside in natural spaces is worth considering as an ongoing daily filler for your happiness sandwich.

3. Music

Anyone who has ever listened to music will tell you, we don't just hear it, we feel it. Rousing songs uplift us. Sad melodies play along with our melancholy. Music creates physical sensations that create emotions. Listening to music can be intrinsically rewarding for the brain, by engaging our reward systems to anticipate what's coming next and all the pleasurable sensations that evokes. Music also creates emotions by stirring memories. Pulp's 'Common People' will always make me dance with joy like I am in a music festival in the middle of a forest, where I first heard the song live. We also find meaning in songs and lyrics that help us normalize, understand and process our feelings. Then there's what we do when we hear music – singing at the top of our voice in the car, dancing in the kitchen, moving and using our body and brain in ways that make us feel good. Music is a simple yet powerful filler.

4. Play, fun and laughter

Play is not just for children. Play, fun and laughter can benefit us all. They are linked to reducing stress, feeling relaxed and other feel-good emotions, and some studies have even linked them to health benefits. What might play look like as an adult? It could be playing games, playing with children, having fun with people you know, learning a dance craze, playing with colour or with the clothes you wear, singing, writing poetry, finding the silliness or ridiculousness in everyday life (I would personally recommend a game of human hungry hippos – google it!). Really, it's about having fun and laughter in any way you can.

5. Rest and breaks

Just keep going, don't give up, what have you done today? We tie productivity and achievement into our worth. Productivity is king, and pausing or resting are for the weak. This is problematic for our happiness – it means we don't pause to break, to reflect, or to just be. We fill the gaps we need to rest by doing more, more, more. All these productive activities require energy, activating the body's drive system, revving our body up for action (I'll speak about this system more later, see page 125). Yes, this might bring us a sense of achievement, meaning and even joy. But too much of this revving up pushes the system out of balance. Long-term activation of the system without rest and recuperation leads to stress, which has a negative impact on happiness and health. We need to balance our body in a way that is beneficial for our health and happiness. We need to see rest, breaks, relaxation and pause as productive in themselves. And they are; for when we do these things, we help our body and brain switch off that revved-up response, and balance it by downregulating. We engage our rest and digest system, which helps restore energy and allows our bodies to physically recover. In fact, studies show we tend to be more productive if we stop and take time out.

The most obvious break for our body and brain is sleep, and it's fundamental to our health, happiness and wellbeing. If you are experiencing sleep difficulties, these should be targeted as a priority. However, incorporating rest and relaxation regularly is important as a happiness sandwich filler. Think about points in your day to pause, slow down, and let your body and mind rest.

6. Curiosity and learning

Curiosity may have killed the cat, but it also sparked up your brain, bringing it alive and making it grow (literally) – shifting it from its existing patterns of neuron connections and forging fresh pathways to incorporate new information. Your brain thrives on learning.

Learning can also give you focus, meaning and a sense of achievement and create positive emotions of pride, joy and relaxation. All in all, learning is good at making us feel good. I don't necessarily mean sitting exams or doing courses – being curious is about the day-to-day learning you add to life. It can be learning about people, finding new places to walk or trying new hobbies. Curiosity is having an open mind that lets you learn new information, and your brain will love you for it.

7. Food and drink

Food can create emotions in many ways, both good and bad. Yet, if we strip it back to its basics, food provides us with the energy for our brain and body to function in the first place. Although I've included it here as a filling, food and drink are also the base of your sandwich as they provide the energy and building blocks to add all the other fillings. A dehydrated and hungry brain is never a happy brain. Once we have the energy we need, we can start to think about food and drink as a filling in itself, as it can create pleasure, help us pause, and give us connections and structure to our day. We can fine-tune how we use food to build happiness, by pausing to eat, increasing our intake of nutrients, or tweaking how and when we eat. Of course, food and drink can also become a false filling in a number of ways – for example, when we drink too much as a coping strategy. Building happiness is also about managing negative associations with food, as this can reduce negative feelings and increase feel-good emotions. (I've added some resources in the Further Reading section if you want to consider your relationship with food further – see pages 188-9.)

EXERCISE 2

Tiny pockets of joy

It's important for your health and happiness to include things on a regular basis that create feel-good emotions, and this exercise is designed to help you plan these small daily things. Use the prompts in the illustration on page 66 to plan pockets of feel-good emotions into your day. I've suggested adding three, but you can do as many as possible! If you are finding this hard, identify the barriers to doing this (the exercise on page 41 may help) and think about how you can manage these.

A tale of two difficult Emotions

ignore · suppress · berate · shame · forbid

Now I feel even worse

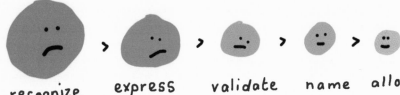

recognize · express · validate · name · allow

Navigating difficult emotions

We know by now that constant happiness is impossible to achieve, and we will all experience difficult emotions in our lives. This means happiness is equally dependent on how we navigate and respond to difficult emotions. Emotions are the language we use to describe how we feel. Our basic feelings can be categorized on two scales – pleasant to unpleasant, and activated to deactivated. Our emotional descriptions are used to identify and explain these feelings. All feelings have a function. For example, feeling fear when we prepare to do something big, such as a job interview, helps the body direct its energy towards getting ready. Feeling sad in response to a life event helps us reflect on it, process it, and seek comfort. Feelings and emotions are meant to ebb and flow, both the good and the not-so-good ones.

While we all experience the same range of underlying basic feelings, the extent to which you feel these and when you experience them will differ. Your brain predicts how to respond to events based on its experiences. For example, if you have had bad experiences with relationships, then your brain will predict that you need to be wary of future relationships. There is never just one emotion for set life events. What makes one person ecstatically happy might make another incredibly scared. You may have a multitude of possible emotions in response to any given situation.

You cannot usually control which emotions arise, as this will happen automatically. Yet we all try to do it. We notice we are feeling scared and we push it away. We feel sad and we tell ourselves to just get on with things. These responses are important. While we can't necessarily decide the way we want to feel at any particular time, we can make decisions about how we respond to our emotions, and the nature of these responses is crucial for our wellbeing and happiness.

Let's start with noticing emotions. We may not want to feel them, but noticing them seems to help us navigate them. Becoming friends with your emotions involves both attention and language. Firstly, we need to notice what is happening in our body – where are our feelings at right now, and how are they affecting us? Secondly, what are these emotions? Categorizing and naming them helps us understand them. The more specific we can be, the more it helps. Research indicates that people who can finely distinguish their negative feelings were more able to regulate their emotions.

So, you've spotted that emotion and tamed it by naming it. That brings us to control. None of us want to feel bad and it's the most natural thing in the world to want to retreat from negative feelings. However, in what's called an 'ironic process', if you tuck these emotions away, it seems to make them want to fight back. The research tells us that trying to suppress emotions increases physiological markers of stress.

Conversely, expressing these emotions helps process them. By expressing them in a way that is helpful to you, you look at them from a different angle, form a comprehensive story about them, and integrate them with other information in your brain, rather than being tied closely to the emotional parts of your brain. Expressing and processing emotions can take different forms – allowing yourself to think about it, speaking it through or even writing it down.

Then there are our beliefs about emotions, which are like the directors for our actions and thoughts when these emotions occur. They are built through the stories we are told during our lifetime, and often our childhood stories are particularly important. If we believe that certain emotions are 'good' or 'bad', this can impact on how we judge ourselves when they occur, how accepting we are of experiencing these emotions and, therefore, what we do when they arise. Studies suggest that acceptance of emotions longer term has been shown to benefit psychological health. Finally, if we feel there are tangible things we can do (which there are, on the following pages!) when we experience emotions, this makes us feel better than if we believe they are out of our control.

These exercises are designed to help you think about how you respond to difficult emotions when they occur.

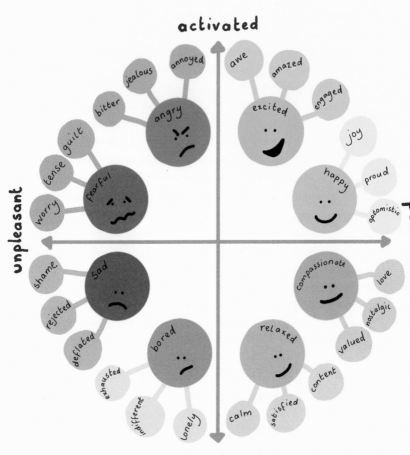

Awareness and categorization

Use the diagram to help you notice how you are feeling. Which category does your feeling fall into, and which emotion labels describe how you feel? These labels are not exhaustive and you might want to think about other labels you can use. You can use a range of labels or as many as you wish to describe how you feel.

Expressing and processing emotions

Think about how you respond to emotions when they occur. Do you hide them, suppress them or tuck them away in a box? Why is this? Unpacking difficult emotions that have been in a box for a long time can be challenging, so consider looking at this with a professional, if there are complex things in that box. However, on a day-to-day basis, when emotions occur, consider how you can express and process them. Here are some ideas that may help:

- *Write down how you feel.*

- *Speak through your emotions with a trusted person.*

- *Think through what you felt and what you can do about this.*

- *Draw a diagram of factors contributing to the emotions.*

- *Draw how you feel.*

- *Write a story of how you feel.*

focusing here can make you feel stressed, uncertain + out of control

Out of my Control

what happened in the past

What other people think

Other people's behaviour

Exactly what will happen in the future

Some external stressors

In my Control

My actions

How I respond to my emotions

How I treat others

Taking care of myself

Setting my boundaries

Living within my values

focusing here can help you plan, problem solve + feel in control

Controlling happiness

At each and every point in life, we have an overwhelming amount of information coming at us. If we tried to process it all, our brain would feel out of control, so it uses shortcuts to find patterns in random data, process it quickly and predict what's coming, so it feels more in control. While your brain is doing all this perpetually on a micro level, you are also doing this from a wider perspective, thinking about what will happen next – today, tomorrow, next year and beyond – so you can plan for it and create meaning. Why do we do this? So that we have a sense of control in the world, amid the unpredictability of life, which makes us feel good.

While we differ individually in how much control we need to feel, we all as humans attempt to exert it over our world. Before online calendars, the one thing that was sure to set me off into panic mode was losing my diary. My brain did not like this one little bit, it sensed the threat and headed off into Panicland. Routines, structuring our days, to-do lists – they all give us a sense of control. Planning for the future does the same; we are, effectively, controlling massive uncertainty by predicting what we think will happen. When the Covid-19 pandemic set in, it made us feel out of control in a number of ways, but partly because it stripped away the illusion of certainty about the future. We really did not know what was going to happen next and we could not plan for it.

To some extent, we all like to know what we are doing. Uncertainty can feel uncomfortable. For example, not knowing what you are doing at work makes you feel doubtful and creates stress. As we've seen, having a sense of control when you experience emotions, knowing you can do something about them, seems to make us more tolerant of them and less likely to suppress them. Experimental studies show that people feel less stressed when they know something bad is happening, like an electric shock, than when they are not sure if it is going to happen. Uncertainty creates stress, because we feel less able to predict what is happening and we often fill the gaps in our knowledge with worry or incorrect information. Ultimately, uncertainty is more demanding for our brain, as it can't take the usual shortcuts to process information quickly and make quick decisions.

Although a sense of agency can make us feel good, like all things, this can sometimes go wrong. If we rely too much on control, and we conflate being in control with our worth, then any little slips can make us doubt ourselves. A good example of this is when children enter our life. Expecting more control than we have in particular situations, for example child birth, can lead to unrealistic expectations and impact negatively if things don't turn out as planned (and they often don't). Trying to control our emotions by suppressing them can be detrimental to how we feel. We may avoid situations that make us feel out of control because they are unknown, when if we did them, they would in fact add to our happiness. Getting stuck in our own viewpoint to avoid feeling out of control can stop us learning, and prevent us from shifting away from belief systems that are unhelpful to us.

When life throws events at us that make us feel out of control, it can make us feel bad. When we have too many stressors in our life, the sense of being out of control, or not being able to do anything about them, creates stress. When massive challenges come into our world, we often have difficulty making sense of these within our existing frame of reference and, therefore, are unsure how to respond. This can pull the carpet from beneath our belief systems, and can make us feel hugely uncertain about what we thought we knew or who we are as people even! Living with uncertainty, such as living through a global pandemic, creates stress in the brain as it uses resources and energy to try and make sense of this information and find solutions, when often there aren't any.

The exercises here are two-fold. They are designed to help give you a sense of control when things feel out of control, and to tolerate those feelings of uncertainty.

Routine

Having a degree of routine in life can be beneficial for giving the brain a sense of predictability and control. Routine is less taxing for the brain because it happens automatically – we don't need to think about it. The level of structure in your life will be down to individual preference, but there are certain areas in which I would recommend a level of routine:

• *A bedtime routine is very helpful to indicate to your brain that it's time to start to switch off, and can help you get to sleep.*

• *A routine for the end of the working day can help – for example, writing a list of what needs to be done the next day, or creating a way to switch between a work and home brain, such as a walk.*

• *Structuring your future time helps reduce cognitive load and stress. I love a diary, but any way you can structure your future time is helpful. Schedule in things to look forward to, as this helps you anticipate the reward, which makes us feel good.*

• *Try thinking about how you can add routine into your life helpfully. Which routines do you enjoy?*

Cognitive flexibility

Novelty and change are the norm in life rather than the exception, so it's beneficial to our wellbeing to be able to manage the unpredictable and adapt when we need to. Having an open mind and being able to shift our thinking when things don't go as planned is sometimes called psychological or cognitive flexibility. Cognitive flexibility is also having awareness that every problem or situation has a number of solutions or responses. Flexibility is important in allowing us to adapt to a continuously changing environment. Yet, ironically, this can create discomfort, as stepping outside what we know means we feel less certain. We can get stuck in one way of thinking, or seeing only one solution, despite it creating unrealistic expectations and often being unhelpful to our wellbeing. Allowing yourself to see multiple courses of action and outcomes can feel uncomfortable in the short term, but can pay dividends for your happiness longer term. Here are some prompts to widen flexibility:

• *Think about other ways to view a situation or problem. How might other people think if they were in the same situation?*

• *Ask for different viewpoints and ideas for work tasks or other tasks that you are problem-solving or feel stuck with.*

• *Instead of dismissing views that are different to yours, listen and enquire further about why people think that or hold a certain opinion (you don't have to agree to understand).*

• *When a situation doesn't go as expected, instead of being stuck on your planned response, stop and rethink the next possible options in light of the new information.*

• *Be open to saying 'I don't know', instead of feeling you have to give an answer or solution.*

Tolerating uncertainty – the worry tree

Often uncertainty feels like a threat, which means the brain tries to resolve and understand the unknown, in an attempt to create certainty. This can result in us filling the unknown gaps unhelpfully, predicting the worst-case scenario, or seeking certainty in places we will never find it, such as Googling the answers, finding out more and more information (like watching the news endlessly during the pandemic) or seeking reassurance. While these may provide short-term reassurance, in the longer term they can make us feel worse as we never deal with the uncertainty itself. Categorizing your thoughts around uncertainty can help you decide how to deal with it, and this exercise is designed to help with this. Use the pathway up the tree opposite to identify your worries and find ideas to deal with them.

Focusing on things you can control

Let's face it, even at the best of times, there is much in our world that is out of our control. While we can't always control what life throws at us, we do have the ability to focus on things that are important to us that we can influence. Use the image on page 80 to categorize what is in your circle of control and what isn't. Focus your attention and resources on tackling those issues within your circle of control and find different ways to manage other worries (see the worry tree exercise above).

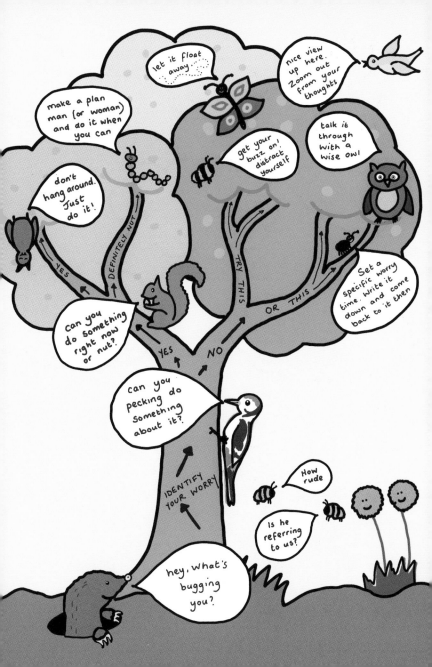

Chapter 3
Perceiving Happiness

Now that we've looked at what makes us happy – our fillings – let's move on to think about other aspects that influence our happiness sandwich. Our beliefs and resulting thoughts contribute to our happiness, as they guide what we put in our sandwich, influencing our behaviour, but can also contribute directly to how we feel. We're also going to shift our thoughts to focus on attention itself. We have limited attentional capacity, and where this is directed determines what is brought to our awareness and, therefore, is added to our happiness sandwich. The brain's natural attentional pull might not always help with building happiness. These two factors interact closely, because our beliefs help the brain decide what we focus on in the environment, as it's drawn to what (it thinks) it knows. We'll look at when our beliefs and attention work against us, and how we can shift them so they help, rather than hinder, our happiness. You can use the happiness sandwich template on page 15 to record your ideas for how to focus your attention and beliefs to foster happiness.

Redefining Success

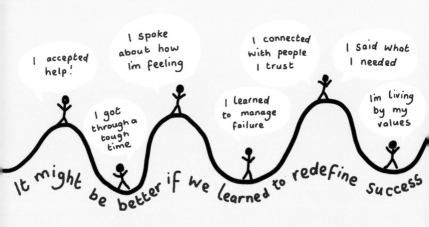

Believing in happiness

People say 'seeing is believing', but to your brain, believing is seeing. Your brain has a set of belief systems it uses to structure, understand and predict the world; these are your stories that underpin your life. The brain bases these stories on the knowledge it has gained through experience – in other words, what it thinks it knows. This can become problematic, because if you think you know something, you pick up evidence to back up your belief. If I believe that I'm a rubbish clinical psychologist, then I will notice every single incident that backs this up. Remember we spoke about the brain being great at processing lots of information quickly? Well, it is great, but your beliefs are central to the shortcuts it takes to do this.

One such example is a day when you've done 211 things well, but one thing didn't go quite so well. Your brain will focus on the one perceived failure. 'It's a total disaster! You get everything wrong!' In reality, it's not a big deal. You've done loads of things well today, and that should have provided lots of information that you are quite decent. It really isn't a disaster, so what on earth is your brain doing?

When your brain believes something, it is tuned into that information and has a spotlight out searching for it in the sea of information that hits your perception. This shortcut is called 'confirmation bias'. One of my favourite psychology studies gave two groups of people with opposing views the same neutral article – and guess what, both groups thought it confirmed their view. Their attention shone its spotlight on the information that seemed to confirm what they believed. Sometimes these brain shortcuts serve us well, so we can quickly understand what's going on. However, sometimes, particularly if our patterns of beliefs are strongly held and unhelpful to us, this brain shortcut doesn't work quite so well.

If the belief is negative, then your brain functioning is a bit like the answer to a bad joke: what do you get when you cross confirmation bias with negative bias? From years of clinical experience, I would suggest the answer to this is your brain takes an exponential leap to become a negative stealth ninja, hunting out all the negative confirmatory evidence, often when there is none.

We have beliefs about many things. We have inane beliefs about inanimate objects (I didn't believe bananas could be frozen until I was in my 30s, and I still feel remorse for all those brown bananas that ended up in the bin). We have beliefs we don't even like to admit to, but study after study shows we have implicit bias that contributes to racism, sexism and many other -isms out there. And, of course, we have beliefs about happiness itself (hopefully realistic ones after reading Chapter 1!). If we zoom out from the specific beliefs and capture the essence as a whole, psychologists like to think of these belief systems as 'constructs' through which we understand our world, which can broadly be defined as a triad of constructs about ourselves, other people and the world.

How do these belief systems develop? From the information that enters our brain; and when that enters as our constructs and brain are developing it appears to be particularly potent. Early attachments and experiences help form the brain itself and shape our belief systems. These are not static – brains and beliefs change beyond our early years – but it can be hard to override constructions of our world that exist in our brain, particularly if these are very powerful or very negative. From a clinical perspective, if you have experienced damaging or difficult experiences, help is often required to step back from the powerful impact these can have on your belief systems. Even when you can step back, if your brain needs to use the easiest, most powerful shortcuts (as it does, for example, when stressed), then it can tend to fall back into these old patterns easily.

I'm not going to pretend that the exercises here will unpick all those subtle belief systems integrated in your brain, but you can start to notice them and what they are telling you. This means you can question their validity, help your brain find instances that are inconsistent with them and begin to shape new beliefs.

Rewriting stories about ourselves

When we talk about self-worth, we are talking about the beliefs we have of ourselves and how these impact on our behaviour. Happiness is linked to the belief that we are equal to others and of value. This exercise is designed to examine these beliefs and shift the outdated ones. Please be cautious with this exercise if you have strong negative beliefs about yourself. Do not use this in an attempt to unpack things you have tucked away for a long time, as this often needs to be done gradually in a safe space.

Step 1: **Noticing you are stuck in your story**

Beliefs are only one way of seeing the world, so we could say that they are just stories that we tell ourselves about who we are, what we can and can't do, and our place in the world. When we get stuck inside a story, we can get stuck in patterns of limiting beliefs or responses that may impact on our happiness. For example, if we tell ourselves, 'I'm not an X sort of person' or 'I'm too old to try new things', we can close off possibilities that we may enjoy. However, we can spot these out-of-date stories we tell ourselves. Start by writing down your response to this:

I believe I am…

• *What, if any, negative words are in there? Would you ever use this label for someone else? Do you think this is a fair way to describe yourself?*

• *Is it something you used to be told? Do you really believe this, or is it an outdated belief your brain still throws at you?*

• *What examples do you have that reinforce this negative belief? Can you think of any other examples inconsistent with this?*

• *What do you honestly think that someone who knew you well would say if you told them this?*

Step 2: **How do these negative beliefs impact your actions?**

For example, if we believe we are incompetent, we might work extra hours to keep up and hide our 'failings'. Consider any ways that these beliefs impact on what you do.

Step 3: **Rewriting your story**

When you engage the critical thinking part of your brain, what do you really think? How would you really describe yourself? If you are feeling brave, ask a trusted person whose opinion you value how they would describe you. This is only advised with people you feel safe with. We are not looking for self-adoration here, but we do want to note that you are just as good, valuable, fallible, worthy, imperfect and as significant as anyone else. Consider how you can respond helpfully when you notice unhelpful beliefs pop up. Could you, for example, say: 'I'm telling myself I'm incompetent, however, this is just a feeling based on an outdated belief system and the stories I tell myself resulting from this'? Remind yourself about your updated belief. For example: 'I am a human that makes mistakes. This doesn't mean I am incompetent.' Use the illustration on page 95 to remind yourself of your out-of-date beliefs and your updated beliefs, which are your new stories for living your life.

Beliefs about success

Beliefs about success drive our behaviour and contribute to incorrect predictions about what will make us happy. Often our beliefs about success are driven by what society has told us, rather than thinking about what success really means to us. Use the image on page 90 to challenge these ideas and think about your new success metrics, then note these down below. Notice when you are being driven by old metrics of success – 'I'm not paid as much as my friends, that means I'm a failure' etc. Instead, use your new metric: 'I'm taking time to look after my mental health, do things that make me happy and spend time with people I care about. What a big success!'

what does success really mean to you?

Write your new metrics of success in the speech bubbles

Compassionate Happiness

Compassion and happiness

Remember that stealth brain ninja, hunting down all the information that fits with those negative beliefs? Well, if you decided to have a chat with it, you'd find it to be negative and critical. It assumes it's speaking the truth, when it is actually casting its judgement in a massively subjective way. We nearly all have a version of this inner negative ninja that is generally critical, making harsh judgements about us and what we do from deep inside the inner workings of our brain. Fuelled by negative bias, the ninja's critical judgements affect your thoughts, your body's stress response, your emotions, your behaviour and how you interact with the world.

However, I'm not going to suggest dismissing your ninja outright – this would make it angry and fight back stronger, and you really don't want to fight with a ninja, do you? Instead, I'm going to argue that you treat it with compassion, be gentle on it and understand it, because this helps calm your ninja and helps it start to see another point of view. Compassion is a far more powerful response to difficult thoughts, feelings and beliefs than fighting against them.

Self-compassion is about being non-judgemental and respectful to ourselves, and is a tool we can use with our beliefs, emotions and behaviours. It helps us understand them, respond usefully and navigate them. Compassion allows us to see our flaws and failings not as personal indicators of our worth, but instead as part of being human. It shifts our pursuit for perfection, allowing us to recognize that perfection is impossible, and that imperfection is normal and inevitable. It allows us to have emotions and experience these without shaming ourselves. Overall, it shifts our thoughts from harsh judgement and self-criticism to understanding and kindness.

Compassion is an important part in the happiness picture in a number of ways. It helps us navigate difficult emotions, as being self-compassionate may reduce how much we suppress emotions and help us be more accepting of them. Greater self-compassion is also linked to less anxiety, stress and depression. It may also benefit our relationships, as it has been linked to a feeling of greater connection to those around us. Compassion may also allow us to meet our goals: people who treat themselves with compassion are more likely to believe they can improve, correct mistakes and re-engage with goals when things go wrong. In contrast, self-criticism is linked to procrastination, stress and rumination – none of which motivate people to continue pursuing a goal nor helps with happiness.

Additionally, compassion may also protect us from the difficult impact that life can have on us. As we know, criticism sets off our stress mechanisms, resulting in a cascade of responses in brain and body, which over the long term is detrimental to happiness. Conversely, compassion seems to help reduce stress and instead engage the body's relaxation system, helping deactive the threat system and regenerate and heal the body.

So, what is compassion and how can you incorporate it in your life to help with your happiness? Kirsten Neff, one of the key researchers of compassion, describes three parts to it: kindness, common humanity and mindfulness (I highly recommend her website if you want to read more, which is listed in the Further Reading section, pages 188–9). Firstly, it involves looking at what your inner brain ninja is telling you and responding with kindness rather than judgement. Secondly, it's about seeing difficult experiences, emotions and distress as part of common humanity, rather than thinking they make you somehow different, which can be isolating. Thirdly, it's about mindfulness, being aware of how you are feeling and how you can respond helpfully to this.

These exercises aim to develop self-compassion. I often receive feedback from people that they can seem a bit cheesy or artificial, and I can identify with that. However, once people try them, they often enjoy them more than they expected. So, this is one of those instances where it's worth setting those predictions aside and giving it a go.

Developing self-compassion

Ask yourself what you need in difficult situations:

1. How would you treat a friend?

Firstly, think about how you would treat a friend or someone you care about going through a difficult time. Would you make harsh judgements about them for feeling bad? Do you think worse of them for experiencing difficult emotions or getting things wrong?

2. How do you treat yourself?

Now think about how you would treat yourself in the same situation. What do you say to yourself? What do you do?

3. Spot the difference.

Is there any difference between the two? Could you imagine treating a friend like you treat yourself? Which of these is more helpful? What do you need in difficult situations?

4. Develop self-compassion.

What can you do in difficult situations to be compassionate to yourself? What can you say to yourself that would be helpful? Think about what you would like to hear in difficult situations to make you feel good and proactively come up with phrases you can say to yourself. Consider what you would want children to hear in these situations or what would have been helpful for you to hear as a child. Start to notice what you say to yourself or do when difficult events or emotions crop up, and try to use these nurturing helpful responses instead. This can be difficult to implement when you most need it (as this is often when your inner critic is at its strongest), so you could use the image on page 98 as a prompt. Alternatively, you could carry a small credit card-sized prompt of nurturing responses to remind yourself.

5. Act consistently with your needs.

Instead of beating yourself up when you feel bad, ask yourself what you need in this situation. Act and speak to yourself in a way that is consistent with your needs and how you would treat a friend or child.

A short compassion pause

This is a quick exercise to incorporate all three parts of self-compassion. If you find this hard to do or initiate by yourself, there are several short meditations online that can help. Tara Brach's RAIN of Self-Compassion Meditation is a very nice and memorable exercise and there are many others on Kristin Neff's website (see Further Reading, pages 188–9). You can use the following exercise when you feel stressed or just at regular intervals throughout your day or week.

• *Stop, breathe slowly, and take notice of how you feel.*

• *Name your feelings, validate them (you can use the Common Humanity image for this – see page 105).*

• *Now what do you need to nurture or soothe you? Respond to yourself with kindness through what you say and what you do.*

Recognizing the common humanity of experiences

When we go through tough times, it can make us feel different and as if we are not responding how we should be. Societal beliefs about emotions and happiness have a part to play here – we believe we should be coping and happy all the time, when that is unrealistic. Common humanity is about recognizing difficult emotions and suffering as a part of life – something we all experience that binds us together rather than separating us.

Start by noticing when you are judging your emotions, responses and experiences. You may be telling yourself that it's not normal to feel like this, that nobody else feels this way, or just calling yourself odd. It could be more subtle, like saying 'I should be coping' or 'other people cope better than me'. These statements make you feel different and isolate you. Use the range of statements in the image opposite to remind yourself that suffering, difficult emotions and distress do not make you different. They are part of what connects you to other people, because they are fundamentally part of the human experience. You may want to come up with your own statements to remind yourself of this when you notice those judgemental and isolating thoughts – and you can add these to the image too.

Zooming Out from your thoughts

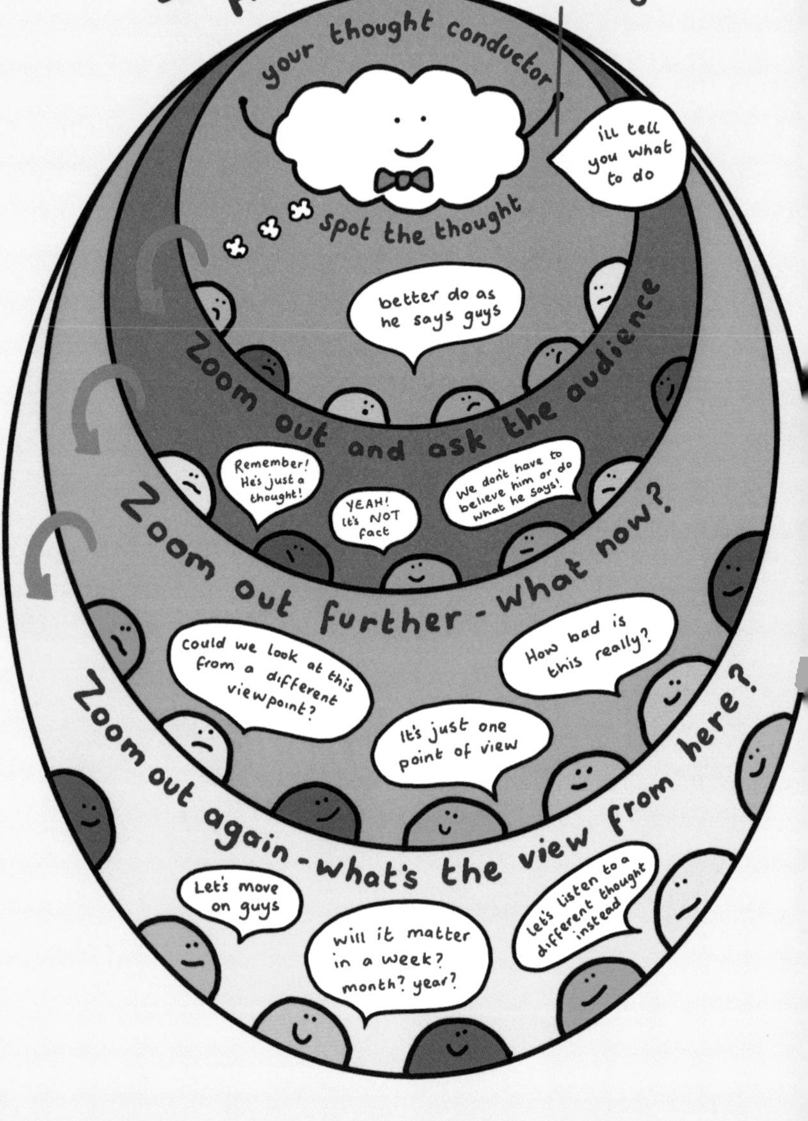

Thinking about happiness

We have thousands of thoughts per day, passing through our brains like trains. Thoughts are constructed by the linking together of information in the brain, which provides structure and understanding for all the sensory information coming at you. These thoughts are an important part of happiness, as they can be seen as the conductor of events. There is a lot of noise happening in our environment, and how this makes us feel depends on how we perceive and interpret it, and that's often down to the thoughts we have about it. These thoughts are interpreting the music of our life and conducting how we respond and interact with it. They are conducting the orchestra (well, you) to feel and behave in a certain way. Just as a conductor interprets the music in a certain way, your thoughts are interpretations of the music in your environment too.

We know that the conductor's interpretation often arises from those internal constructs, our 'belief systems', to affect our feelings and behaviours. Digging down into the belief system can be hard, but spotting its by-product, our thoughts, can often be easier, and is something we can notice and respond to. Sometimes there's great synchronicity between all our conductors. Some life events are difficult and will create sad music for nearly everyone. But across most of life, there's great variability in how we interpret events and what is produced from it. Person 1 may see a failed exam as something terrible that means they will never achieve for the rest of their life, let alone be happy. Person 2 may be annoyed that they've failed, but interpret the failed exam as a one-off event. Person 3 decides that this is an indicator that this course is not right for them and they need to choose a different path. Because of a range of factors, including what's currently happening in their life, their experiences to date and their internal belief systems, each person's conductor has interpreted the same event differently. None are wrong, but none are factual either.

However, just because your conductor interprets one life event a particular way doesn't mean that's how it will always be. Once you become aware of the conductor, they are more open to change than you might think. Now, I'm not saying that you can slap a 'just think positive' badge on your conductor, because these thoughts often arise automatically. Importantly, it's not all about being positive, rather it's about recognizing thought patterns and how these influence how we feel and what we do. Rather than dismiss it, we need to listen to our conductor's initial interpretation, but – and this is key – we don't need to believe it or agree with it. We can step back, zoom out and consider alternative interpretations, think about which parts are unhelpful to us or consider whether there is another interpretation to guide the orchestra in another, more helpful direction.

What about conducting happiness? Are there thoughts or interpretations of events that are more conducive to happiness and wellbeing? The answer is yes. Firstly, being able to spot your conductor is there in the first place and what it is telling you is beneficial. This allows you to zoom out and look to the audience to consider if there are any other interpretations. As there is normally a large audience listening to an orchestra, there are many different ways of interpreting the music. Secondly, being open to the views of the audience, allowing your conductor and your thoughts to be flexible, allows you to see more ways of responding apart from the one you've always known. Thirdly, the conductor's interpretation (the content of your thoughts) is important. As we saw when we looked at compassion, judgemental and critical thoughts are stressful for brain and body, and make us want to hide rather than face the music.

But there is another set of responses that have been identified as beneficial to wellbeing. Sometimes this is called an 'optimistic explanatory' style of thinking. If optimism seems a stretch too far, another take on this, as coined by the writer and philanthropist Hans Rosling, is that this is a 'possibilist' thinking style, as it helps you find ways forward and solutions at difficult times. Optimism can feel unrealistic, but thinking of it as an open and realistic style of thinking, which allows for more flexibility and considers possibilities, seems more achievable.

An optimistic (or possibilist, if you prefer) explanatory style means difficult events are more likely to be viewed as External (they are not all your fault), Inconstant (they do not reliably predict the future) and Specific (they do not determine your entire life). When difficult events happen, people with these explanatory styles are less likely to blame themselves, or view the events as permanent or pervasive in their lives. The contrasting explanatory thinking style, sometimes called helplessness (because it makes us feel helpless), would explain the event as Internal (blame yourself), Permanent (unchangeable) and Stable (determines your entire life).

The explanatory style we use is important. An optimistic explanatory style is associated with happiness, as well as adaptation to stress and recovery from difficult events. It is also associated with better health, longer lifespan and greater odds of achieving 'exceptional longevity' – that is, living to the age of 85 or beyond. But can we influence our thinking style? There's evidence that people can learn and adapt their explanatory style to be more beneficial to them. It's certainly an intervention I've seen work first hand in a clinic.

The following exercises aim to help you identify thinking styles that can be unhelpful for your happiness and instead develop thinking styles that are compatible with happiness.

Zooming out from your thoughts and listening to the audience

This exercise is designed to help you zoom out from your original unhelpful interpretations of an event to look at it from different perspectives. Use the illustration on page 106 to firstly, identify what your thought conductor is telling you, then zoom out from the thought in stages using the questions and statements from the audience to scrutinize it. Do you really need to believe the thought or can you come up with other ways of looking at the situation?

We might have an interpretation we are driven to naturally, as it derives from our longstanding belief styles, which may in fact be seriously biased or unhelpful. Yet, we can step back from our original thoughts and see which ones we want to engage with to lead the orchestra and design our life.

The focus of your thoughts is important, too, because where your conductor focuses your thought, and the extent to which you get stuck in this focus, can impact on how you feel. If the conductor is focusing on a song called 'Rumination Across the Nation', he is stuck on the past, going over and over this, with no solution, getting tied in knots thinking about it. Your conductor might also get caught in future-focused thought, in a song called 'It's a Catastrophe', and spend all his time filling the unknown gaps of the future with worries, coming to no conclusions and to the detriment of the music in the here and now. Try exercise 3 on page 112 or the worry tree exercise on page 87 if you notice your thought conductor doing this.

Developing an optimistic/possibilist explanatory style

This exercise is designed to help you consider if there is a better way to explain a stressful or difficult event. Note down ways of looking at the situation, using the questions to think about this.

Am I interpreting this situation in any of these ways?

Can I see the situation from this perspective instead?

<u>Internal</u> (blaming myself)

<u>External</u> Am I really all to blame for it? Were there other contributing factors?

<u>Permanent</u> (it will never change)

<u>Inconstant</u> Will this really happen constantly?

<u>Stable</u> (defines or determines your entire life)

<u>Specific</u> Does this one example really define me?

Rumination across the nation

Rumination is a hamster wheel of worry, where we are running round and round without reaching a solution. Instead, we create more worry, anxiety or low mood, which makes us ruminate more. The brain is trying to help us, attempting to understand or to solve our concerns, but this is counterproductive and we are trapped on the hamster wheel with no resolution. Use the illustration to help you identify when you are ruminating and find helpful ways to manage your worries instead.

Noticing happiness

Our attention is crucial for building our happiness sandwich, but it's a limited resource – we can only attend to or carry a certain amount of information in our mind at once. Our attention can be thought of as the point on which our brain focuses its spotlight. Conversely, where it dims its spotlight, we don't notice other information. This also determines what enters our awareness and what we remember – we are more likely to store information if we have given it a good dose of our attention.

The brain needs to manage attention wisely, as there are infinite stimuli that can use it up. Many things affect how and where we allocate our attention, and some have already been touched on in this book. Automatic brain biases draw our attention to negative information. Adaptation means we get used to information, while novelty demands our attention. We need to allocate attention to novel information, to work out what to do with it (is it a danger?), how to safely navigate a new route, or to adapt to change. Our attention tends to be drawn to things that fit with our belief systems and disregards information that doesn't. When information becomes meaningful to us, we spot it more. The classic example of this is that as soon as you are trying to get pregnant, you spot pregnant women everywhere – because it has become meaningful to you.

In our happiness sandwich, how and where we allocate our attention is important. Our beliefs affect what we take in from the environment, but also affect how much attention we pay to our sandwich itself. Will we keep building it and using it, or will demands of life take over so that we forget about the sandwich altogether until it lies languishing at the back of the fridge, doing no good for anybody.

Attention is something we have control over, to some extent. These exercises are designed to help you use your limited resource of attention to maximize your wellbeing and input effectively to your happiness sandwich.

Overriding negative bias

Your attention is pulled towards threat, and negative information demands your attention. Let's take a random – *ahem* – example of an author who just happens to be a psychologist – even if you get hundreds of 5-star reviews, you will be pulled towards that one 1-star review. The negativity will sometimes fill your attention. The same applies to everyday life: you'll mull over that one negative comment about your work, when you had twenty positive ones. Don't beat yourself up even more for doing this – it's a natural brain process. Some research even suggests that all events aren't created equal: we need a ratio of around five positive events to one negative event to make us feel good. Let's step back, notice what is demanding your attention, and think about creating a fair way to distribute your attention and help your brain notice the stuff that will make you feel far, far better.

Here are some ways to help your brain notice the positive, which you might want to consider adding as tools for your happiness sandwich. Everyone is different, so see what works for you.

Reflect on achievements. At the end of your day, or at the end of your work day (in fact, at any time during the day) STOP and pause. Take some time to reflect on what you have achieved or done today. What have you done well? What was difficult that you managed? What are you proud of? I often talk about regularly using a Ta-Da list as the natural partner to your To-Do list to note these things down.

Find the positives. When you notice yourself mulling over something negative, STOP. Think if there is any contradictory information your brain is overlooking. For example, if you are thinking about that slip-up in a meeting, was there anything else that went well today, or any part of the meeting when you spoke fluently? If you shouted at your children, were there any times that went well today? Were there more times you responded calmly?

Take the long view. Reflect at regular longer intervals about what you have done over a period of time. Can you give yourself credit for getting through a tough period? Can you notice some things you feel you did well? It can be helpful to do this both at work and in your personal life.

Notice the good from the day. Remember the moments you enjoyed. Write them down to help you remember, or look at photos. It may help to create some structure around this. Some people like to complete a 'three things I am grateful for today' list. It's a nice way to shift your attention to focus on the good.

Nudge your attention towards the good. Keep a clipboard on your desk with feel-good reminders of positive days or events you are planning. Keep a record of your achievements in sight at work. Pin those 'thank you' cards up! Remember, you stop seeing it once the novelty wears off, so ring the changes to keep your attention on them. Shift items to a new position, add to or change them. You can even use social media or the internet as prompts to help you notice the good by following accounts such as The Happy News, Upworthy or The Good News Movement (also great ways to induce awe!).

Flow

Time perception changes according to what's going on in your life and where your awareness is. Sometimes you may be so caught up in an activity you are focusing on that you forget not only time but also yourself, and everything/everyone around you. Flow is about being completely absorbed in what you are doing in the present. Being in a state of flow feels good. I realized when I started drawing illustrations about people's experiences at the height of the pandemic that this helped me switch off from my daily stressful job in the NHS. In some strange way, drawing other people's concerns became one of my key coping strategies (even when frequently disturbed by home-school children asking for a snack – once again showing the importance of context).

Flow is good for you for several reasons. It engages you and often gives you pleasure and meaning. It helps your brain switch off from worldly demands. Think about times when you have been fully absorbed in what you were doing and you felt good. These are your flow activities. The most commonly described activities which create flow are being creative, being in nature, playing sport or music, but you can experience flow in any activity. You can also increase flow by removing distractions (when possible) and really focusing on what you are doing. Flow activities need the right level of challenge – enough to make it interesting, but not too much to make it a frustrating experience. Note down a list of activities that enable your attention to flow. Consider making time for these activities as often as you can as part of your happiness fillings.

hedonic adaptation:

we get used to good things quickly
and our attention shifts away from them

savouring:

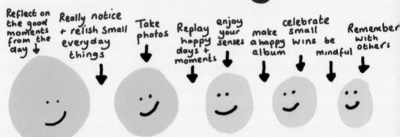

Reflect on the good moments from the day ↓

Really notice + relish small everyday things

Take photos ↓

Replay happy days + moments ↓

enjoy your senses ↓

make a happy album ↓

celebrate small wins ↓

be mindful ↓

Remember with others ↓

these things help us savour good things
so the positive effects last for longer

Savouring happiness

Our negatively-driven brain gets used to good quickly, meaning we adapt to it and shift our attention away from it (remember, this is called 'hedonic adaptation'). Savouring exercises are designed to thwart hedonic adaptation to positive events. Being able to savour the good is associated with happiness by helping you to recall the detail, keeping the good moments in your attention longer and helping you to remember them. There are several ways to do this – some options are shown on the illustration opposite. Think about what savouring tools work best for you and add them to your happiness sandwich.

Being in the here and now

There's a common theme running through the last few attention tasks – to some extent they all require focusing your attention on the present. This helps you notice factors in your environment that make you feel good, and shift thoughts away from worries about the past or the future. Being aware of the moment is linked to helping the body relax, so creates positive sensations and emotions, which we need for happiness. It can also help reduce stress. Mindfulness and meditation are some of the best-known examples, and there are many online meditations and apps that can help you learn this skill. The 'awe walk' earlier in the book (see page 64) is another way of bringing your attention to the present.

Chapter 4
Protecting Happiness

So you've introduced a range of helpful tools to build your perfect happiness sandwich. But hold on, there's a problem – there are risks and threats on the horizon looking for a piece of your sandwich, and we need to protect it from being decimated. The threatening seagull of stress is eyeing up your sandwich, just waiting for the right moment to swoop and grab it out of your hand. The demands in your life, which seem so important at the time, leave you no time to partake in or even notice those happiness fillings that bring you joy. The multiple distractions all vying for your attention distract you from what really matters to you. The weight of other people's judgement makes you doubt your value, what you are doing, and even what you have put in your happiness sandwich. How can you ensure that you don't let these threats to happiness pull your sandwich apart, leaving behind only a soggy lettuce leaf and crusts? These risks exist both internally and externally, so let's look at them in more detail, as well as the tools to manage them.

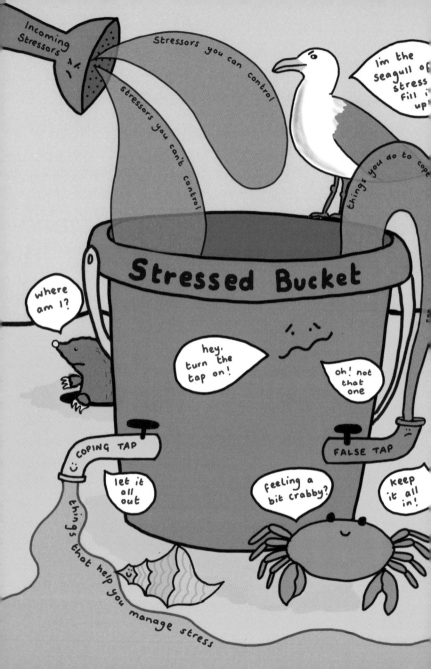

Protecting yourself from stress

The number one risk to your sandwich is that seagull of stress – a constant threat, waiting to snatch it out of your hand. Stress comes from the Latin word *strictus*, meaning 'drawn tight', and anyone who has ever felt their shoulders tense or jaw tighten when they experience stress will know just how apt this meaning is. Stress and its causes can be thought of as the relationship between what's going on in the environment (stressors), our appraisal of these stressors and the resources we have to manage them. When there is too much threat and/or when your perceived demands outweigh your perceived resources, you can feel stressed. Stress is linked fundamentally to how we feel and our bodies, so when we consider its impact, it can be thought of as an imbalance in essential body functions. The balance between the stress/threat response (sympathetic nervous system) and relaxation (parasympathetic nervous system) response is a bit off: there's too much firing up of our body due to activation of our threat system, without enough calming down of our body, which we require to function well.

Stress engages the sympathetic nervous system, which sets off multiple body responses that can affect how we feel both emotionally and in our brain and body functioning, thinking processes and what we do (I eat lots of Pringles

when stressed, it's a sure sign that I have too much on).
Stress is there constantly in our lives to some extent, and in
short bursts that's okay. Sometimes it can even be helpful –
we might need small doses of it to keep us going, to hand in
those university essays or energize us to prepare for that
interview. Our body's stress response gets us ready for action
and ready to deal with the stressor, and that can be a good
thing when we need it.

However, when we have too much stress because we don't
have the capacity to meet the demands in our life, or
threatening stressors continue for too long (sometimes
called chronic stress), this becomes unhelpful to us and a
danger not only for how we feel and our happiness, but also
for our physical health too. Short-term bodily responses to
stress are designed to help, but if the stress doesn't pass
quickly and these responses are firing for too long, they can
be detrimental and damaging.

Stress impacts on wellbeing in a variety of ways. Firstly,
anyone who has ever been stressed (i.e. nearly everyone)
knows it can make us feel terrible. Secondly, the stress
response itself can impact on immune functioning, brain
functioning, and many other physical components of the
body, including arteries, heart and stomach function.
Chronic stress is also a predictor of poor wellbeing and
mental health difficulties. It can disrupt sleep and impact on

energy levels and diet, which make us feel even worse. Furthermore, our well-intended attempts to cope may even be unhelpful to our wellbeing. We might start to drink too much or avoid the stressor. We might feel like we don't have the time to do the things that make us feel good. As a result, those happiness fillers are abandoned, viciously snatched away by the stress seagull.

Recognizing and managing stress is fundamental to happiness and needs to be a priority. Identifying and understanding your stress levels, and the tools you use to manage stress, keep your happiness sandwich intact. I often use the example of the capacity cup to identify when your demands are outstripping your capacity and it's at risk of bubbling over. Another model I like to use is the stress bucket. We can identify when our bucket is becoming full and we are feeling stressed, so we know we need to act. We can also look at the taps filling our bucket – the stressors coming in. We may be able to turn some taps off and manage some of the stressors. Of course, we can't control it all, but we can look at how we manage stressors, helpfully or unhelpfully – the taps we use to reduce our capacity. Some of these may be false taps, which seem to work in the short term but end up refilling your bucket and adding more to your stress. Let's look at this in more detail.

Your stress bucket: identifying its fullness

Use the illustration on page 124 to identify the fullness of your stress bucket. What are the signs it is getting full? Consider behaviour, emotion, physical and thought signs. Do you have clear behaviour signs, things you stop or start doing when stressed (e.g. seriously increased Pringle eating)? What are your emotion signs – things such as irritability, increased tears, or feeling overwhelmed. Physical signs vary but often include: tense muscles, upset stomach, disrupted sleep. Finally, your thought signs might include racing thoughts, difficulty concentrating and more negative thoughts. Spotting your signs helps you identify when you need to be vigilant and act to keep your sandwich safe.

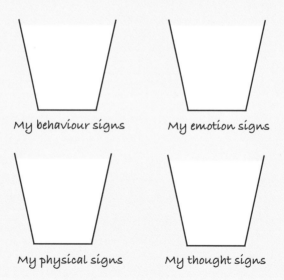

My behaviour signs   My emotion signs

My physical signs   My thought signs

Identify the stressors filling your bucket

What is filling your bucket? Using the image on page 124, classify these into two categories – the stressors you can control and those that you can't. When you are at risk of spilling over, think about which stressors you could stop to help manage your stress and how you might do this.

False and real coping taps

What helps you empty your bucket and cope with stress (a coping tap), and what do you do in an attempt to cope but it actually adds more stress (a false tap)? Coping taps are strategies that are useful to manage stressors. Think about what turns your coping tap on and add it to your stress bucket picture. When you notice your stress rising, consider how you can use your coping taps. Some ideas that have been shown to help include social connections, relaxation, slow breathing, exercise, prioritizing sleep, eating and drinking regularly, talking things through and problem solving.

Now think about what turns your false tap on. What seems like it helps you deal with stress, but longer term just adds to the pile? Often false taps are about avoidance of the stressors. They make us feel good short-term as they distract us from the stressors. However, longer-term, research shows that if avoidance is your main coping style, then this can exacerbate stress.

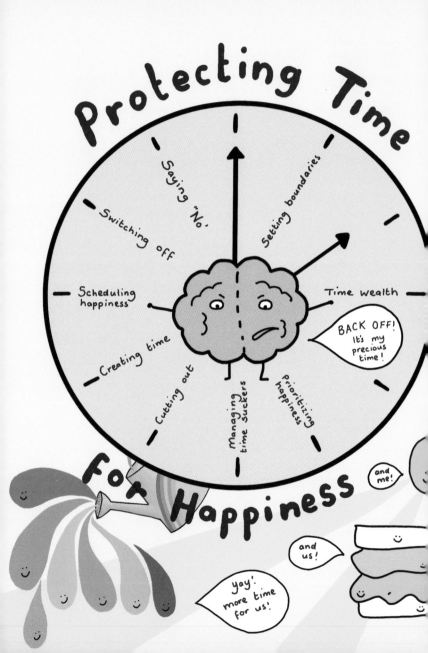

Protecting your time

Time scarcity – feeling like we have no time, particularly no time to do the things that make us feel good – can make us feel pressured and is associated with increased stress, which we know impacts on happiness. Interestingly, studies show that people who value time over money (time wealth over monetary wealth) are more likely to choose rewarding activities and be happier. Yet, when asked, a large proportion of people report that they don't have the time to do what they want to do. If you've ever found yourself committing more time to work than you'd like to, so that it starts impacting on your family time or seeing your friends (or other things that make you happy), then you'll identify with this.

Your time is a precious commodity; I would argue it's the most valuable commodity in your life. The decisions you make about your time can have critical implications for your happiness. We need to think as much about how we spend our time as we think about how we spend our money, and value it more. I don't mean in terms of efficiency and getting lots done, I mean in terms of spending our time well, in a way that is consistent with what makes us feel good, gives us value and meaning, and protects our happiness. Here are some ideas to help you look at time as a precious commodity, using your time in ways that are meaningful to you and conserving your time and associated energy to protect happiness.

Time/happiness analysis

Are there ways to protect your time for the things that you put in your happiness sandwich? Here are some questions you can use as prompts:

• *Which aspects of your time do you have some control over?*

• *Are there things you can reduce so that you have time for things that add to your happiness?*

• *Can you schedule in your happiness fillers to ensure you have time to do them?*

• *Is there anything that is sucking your time away and not making you feel good? For example, are you drawn into your phone or emails at times you don't need to? How could you manage this?*

• *Are there things you need to set boundaries around to help protect your time? For example, being clear about your days of work and not getting drawn into work tasks on non-work days, or putting your phone away when you are doing something enjoyable so you can focus fully on the task in hand.*

• *Are there ways to plan to create pockets of time? For example, can you organize a babysitter in advance, or allocate tasks to other people?*

• *If you can afford to, can you spend to create time? For example, pay someone to clean the windows, cut the grass, take on some admin tasks, do the ironing?*

Protecting your time by saying 'no'

Sometimes we do things we don't want to because we are scared of not doing them or saying 'no'. There are lots of reasons for this: we might be worried we'll offend people or let them down; we might feel that doing these things proves our worth; or we might feel guilty if we don't do them.

Alternatively, sometimes we have lots of nice things coming our way and we want to do them all but realistically just don't have time. Saying no can sometimes feel scary, so we can avoid doing it for fear of repercussions, perhaps upsetting people, or the fear that it will influence how people view us. It's back to those belief systems again that tell us what we should be doing, or not, and create fears that drive our behaviour, which can make it difficult to say no. Long-term beliefs might tell us we need to seek approval or please others. But saying no is a skill and, usually, once we start, we find our fears are unfounded and there are far more benefits to it than downsides. Saying no can help us allocate more time to meaningful things. We can build our happiness sandwich based on what is important to us, rather than trying to fit it in around the things we said yes to because we were worried about saying no.

Try working through the questions on the following pages when you are considering saying 'no'.

What is the decision or request I am having to respond to?

Understanding my initial response:

• *How does this request make me feel? What am I thinking?*

• *Do I feel an urge to agree or say yes?*

• *Do I feel obliged to say yes? Why?*

• *What am I worried will happen if I say no?*

Making the decision:

• *Is this something I want to do?*

• *Is this something I will resent or feel angry about if I say yes?*

• *Will saying yes be helpful or unhelpful for my wellbeing or time?*

• *If unhelpful, am I willing to accept this consequence?*

• *Which decisions fit best with my values and what's important to me?*

• *Will there be any negative consequences if I say no?*

• *What about if I say yes?*

• *What would saying no allow me to do instead?*

• *What would I advise someone else to do?*

My decision:
• *What decision did you come to? Remember, no isn't always negative; it can be a positive choice to enable you to move towards your values, commit time to what's important and make you and those around you happy.*

My response:
• *If you said no, was the response what you expected? Did any of your fears become true? You can use this as evidence to help next time you are dithering about saying no.*

• *It can be helpful to have some thought-out responses to answer these questions, perhaps saved in your email/texts, so you are ready with them when you need to say no.*

• *If you want to take a moment to decide whether to say yes or no, you could use these statements as ideas to give you time to think before responding: 'Could I check my calendar and get back to you?' Or, 'Could you email me that request so I can take a look at it?'*

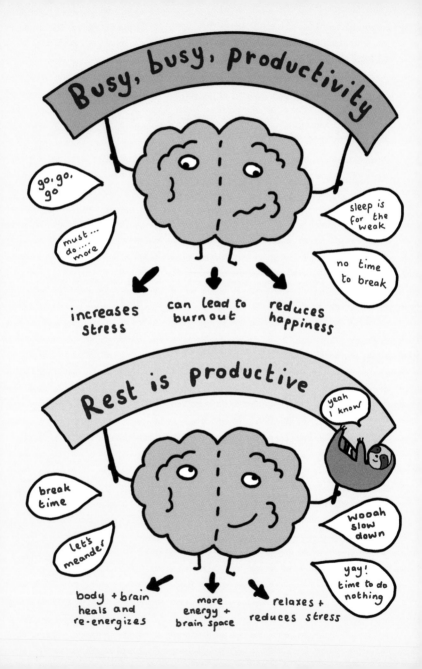

Other risks to your happiness

The need to feel productive, general distractions and the thought of other people's judgement can all impact on your happiness levels. It's important to recognize these threats and consider how you might manage them.

The push for productivity

'I'm so busy!' we chant in unison, buying into the push for productivity, feeling the need to do more, more, more. Feeling we are not achieving if we take a break, filling our diaries until they are overflowing, tying our worth into what we have (and haven't) done, failing to prioritize our needs and seeing stopping as a fundamental flaw.

Woaaah! *STOP*. Slow down, take a breath. Perpetual productivity is counterproductive. We need to recognize that pausing and stopping are productive in themselves. I'm as guilty as the next person of powering through a lunch break to get a task done, but I'm neglecting to realize that this is actually impacting on my health, happiness and productivity. Not only does taking a break make us more efficient long term, it helps our body manage stress by restoring its equilibrium. Let's give downtime the respect it deserves. Rest is not a waste of time; it is so important for health and happiness it needs to have priority status. It's an activity to be planned and appreciated in its own right.

Scheduling downtime

How often do you miss your breaks (like me) or only schedule in downtime as a reward? Planning downtime means it is more likely to happen. Here are some ideas for how to do this:

• **Plan** *Ensure you take all your annual leave. Schedule this in, so you have planned rest periods throughout the year.*

• **Schedule** *Write your lunch breaks and tea breaks into your calendar – block them off as protected time. Plan what you will do in these pockets that will help you relax.*

• **'To-don't' time** *Schedule in protected periods at work or in your personal life when nothing else can be added to your calendar (call them catch up/admin slots, if you must).*

• **Mini breaks** *Get up from your desk every hour. Schedule in time at the end of the day to reflect and plan for tomorrow.*

• **Breathing breaks** *Help calm body and mind: stop, take three slow breaths and gather your thoughts. Then think about what you will do next. This helps regulate your body and manage stress.*

• **Breaks between tasks** *Allow yourself pauses between work meetings, perhaps go for a walk before you start the next task. Try not to over-schedule your day and allow yourself thinking space. Give yourself the gift of space, time and opportunity to pause.*

• **Look up and out** *This is a very simple way to pause and give your brain a break. Look up and out of a window at the horizon, the trees, the buildings around you.*

Other people's perceptions

Often we get caught up in what other people think and the judgements they are, or we perceive they are, making about us. We are social animals, and the brain is designed to imagine what other people are thinking and feeling; sometimes called 'theory of mind'. There have even been neurons identified called 'mirror neurons', which may play a part in feeling and perceiving the emotions and actions of other people. This is an important skill of the brain, as we need this ability to be able to interact effectively and form social groups, which help us be safe, survive and thrive.

Like all amazing brain abilities, this can have a downside. We can get caught up in other people's opinion of us and stop ourselves doing things we want to do in case we are judged. We can all misjudge what people are thinking and misinterpret their responses. If we place too much value in the wrong people's, or too many different people's, opinions, and integrate them into our self-belief and worth, then it can become detrimental to us. We may try to live by others' opinions rather than being guided by what's important to us and our own values.

People judge. We all make judgements because we are basing our opinions on the small bit of information we see, and brain biases drive us to make decisions quickly. Our judgements are also influenced by our belief systems, and we know we are driven to see what we believe. We will all have to face the judgements of others. How can we make sure these judgements don't start to influence us negatively and impact on our happiness sandwich?

I once worked with an amazing person who had a brain injury. People judged him all the time. They thought he was drunk when he walked around shops, they tutted at him as he stood at the shop counter, or beeped as he crossed the road, taking longer than they wanted him to. How did he react? Well, we couldn't rationalize this, because it was clear they were judging. Instead, he said to himself, 'They don't know the whole story', reminding himself that people were making judgements based on small pieces of information and their own beliefs. Of course, this didn't make him immune to judgement – it still upset him sometimes – but he was able to step back and say, 'It's not a judgement about me and it doesn't reflect on me', and separate this from his self-judgements. He was one of the wisest people I've met, and I've carried this with me to this day and use it myself.

So let's look at helpful ways to think about judgements to protect your happiness with the flow chart opposite.

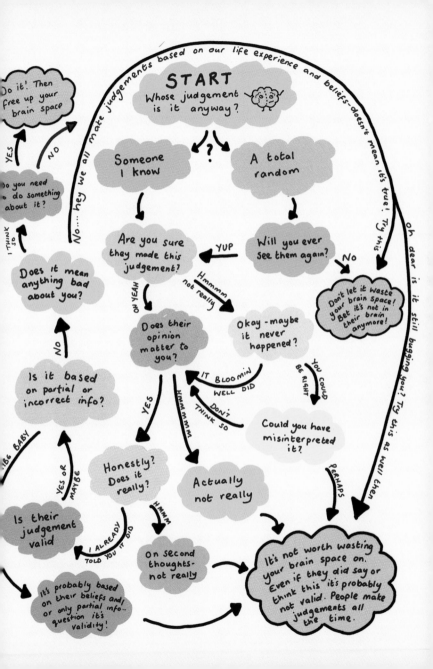

Distractions from happiness

Hey, look at me! No, look at me! What in your environment is demanding attention? What beeps at you mid thought stream, disrupting your flow, so you have to attend to it? I'm pretty sure for most of you I will have conjured up a picture in your mind of technology, most probably your mobile phone or social media. Although there will be other things that distract you, these technologies are designed to draw your attention. Yet, you need to treat your attention with value and not let it get out of your control, at the beck and call of distractions. So, I want to draw your attention to technology's distractive nature (and hopefully away from your emails, Twitter or checking your texts).

Research on the impact of technology on happiness, shows that simply having a mobile phone present at a meal means we enjoy it less. We only have limited attention, so if we allocate more of it to the meal and the conversation of those we are with we will enjoy it more. It's not just meals, technology distracts us from experiencing happiness in a range of places – it stops us being able to focus on what we want to put into our happiness sandwich, and its constant beeping makes us alert, which switches on our stress response. Multitasking with technology is more cognitively demanding and therefore more stressful. If we can reduce multiple demand, we can increase our focus on the task in hand and reduce our stress response.

Removing distraction

Don't rely on motivation to remove distraction...technology is far too clever for that. We simply need to remove distractions so they don't have the same pull on our attention.

Research shows that having a mobile phone in the same room as us draws our attention and uses our focus. Even worse, if it's on the table, we just can't seem to ignore it. So, the best course of action is to put it away. Don't take it on your walk. If you must keep your phone with you but you're able to switch it off, then do. Set limits so you are not on it at certain times. Take the work email off your phone...you are not working at 11pm on a Saturday night, so you don't need it. At the very least, switch off as many notifications as you can, so that you don't have the constant stress-inducing, attention-demanding beeps that impact on your happiness.

Of course, it's not just technology that distracts us, many things do. So you can apply these techniques to them too. Don't trust your motivation or attention to keep you focused, use this diagram to help remove distractions and create barriers to them when you can. Keep your attention – one of the most valuable resources you have – for what really matters.

Chapter 5
Building Happiness

Okay, so now we know the theory behind happiness and which fillings we need in our sandwich. We also know how to input our attention effectively and the tools we need to make our sandwich. Yet this is only part of the story. If we know which path to take and keep on looking down that path but never taking steps on it, it will lead to frustration. We need to take steps in the right direction to build the happiness sandwich and then use it in our lives. This is the output from the sandwich, how we use it, because it is the actions in our lives – what we do on a daily basis – that have the greatest impact on how we feel. Because happiness is not something you obtain, it's something you do and it is the actions you take that build your happiness. To do this, we need to learn to override those brain functions and old habits that keep pushing us down an unhelpful path, and build new actions that are compatible with happiness. However, no matter how much knowledge we have about happiness, or how much we want it in our lives, it's not always easy to achieve. This chapter looks at ways to build longer lasting happiness through our actions.

Habits for happiness

So, now we know what makes us happy, we will be happy. However, it's actually more like this: we know what makes us happy…but despite this, often we don't put the theory into action. Yes, we may have all the skills and knowledge to build our sandwiches effectively, but often we don't then go on to use the sandwich well; it falls apart at the final hurdle – the output stage. I'm going to use myself as an example: why do I (the person who tells you that taking breaks reduces stress and makes you more efficient) sit at my computer eating my lunch while working, to the point where I can't remember if I've even eaten that lunch? I know this is unhelpful for me, so what on earth is going on?

To answer that, I'm returning to our old friend (or perhaps, more accurately, our 'frenemy'), the brain. This behaviour is habit. I didn't always do this; it started at a time of huge pressure when I was training (and it was probably also the cultural norm), and I began eating my lunch at my desk to save time. I did it over and over again until it became habitual to my brain. My brain will choose this route by default, because it is the most learned behaviour. Something in my office context (probably my stomach rumbling) will send a cue to my brain that it's lunchtime, and I will pick up my sandwich and eat it with very little awareness. It is a no-brainer to my brain, it's just what it does.

Habits don't require new learning from the brain; they are stored as a sequence of activities in our sensory motor cortex. The brain adds a routine of behaviours together so they all happen automatically in sequence when triggered by a cue (that rumbling stomach) to get us to a reward (my lunch), which in turn reinforces that learned behaviour. The cue sets off a double whammy of behaviour that I require the help of both Diana Ross and Britney Spears to explain. Before you know it, your brain is 'in the middle of a chain reaction', and once you start, you can't stop (or at least it's difficult to), so you're soon saying, or singing, 'Oops, I did it again' (because your brain will default to this automatically). Your brain uses habits to minimize effort and save energy, and will default to these behaviours when cued.

In order to learn new activities, your brain needs to plan and set a goal, which requires the brain's executive function regions (the manager of your brain) to execute this successfully. Your brain needs to monitor what's going on, track its intentions, inhibit its learned processes, problem-solve and plan. Phew, that sounds exhausting doesn't it? You can see why your brain wants to default to its habits. So, how can we help it shift away from habits that are incompatible with happiness and instead build happiness habits into our lives? Here are some ways to build those habits and help shift the happiness sandwich from theory to action.

Uncover your happiness habit

Step 1: **What is it that you want to do?**

Look at the happiness fillers from your happiness sandwich (see pages 45-9) and decide which you want to add as small daily habits. Next, think about how and when you will do this. Alternatively, consider the habits that are incompatible with happiness and that you want to break. Like me, do you want to stop eating lunch at your desk and get outside instead? Don't just focus on what you don't want to do here, but focus on what you will do as well.

Step 2: **Be clear about your why**

What will you gain from this new happiness habit? Why is it important to you? Consider whether this is one of the moons connecting to your 'why' planets (see page 58). This helps you to want to make the conscious effort to override your default habits.

Step 3: **Be specific**

Decide when specifically you will engage in your new habit and what you will do – for example, 'I want to go for a walk to connect with nature at lunchtime.' Make sure this is manageable. If you set something you can't do, this will not turn into a habit. Start as small as you can, because this is more likely to be achievable, repeatable and rewarding – three things we need to happen to shift from an effortful new behaviour to a habit. Don't overwhelm that poor brain of yours with too much in one go, as it will give up and return to your default natural habits. Start by introducing one happiness habit at a time.

Rework your cues

Step 1: **Set a cue**

Now, I can't get my stomach to rumble on demand, so for my lunch I might set an alarm to remind me to go for a walk. This cue forms the habit and helps my brain to learn a new sequence.

Step 2: **Consider the context**

Have you ever noticed you are more likely to use certain behaviours with certain people or in certain places? Habits are context-specific. So, if you are looking to shift an old habit, consider if you can shift the context. So, using my habit as an example – can I shift the context at lunchtime? Can I arrange to be doing work away from my computer at lunchtime? A change of scenery will reduce the chance of the context cueing the old habit.

Step 3: **Repeat, repeat, repeat**

Repetition turns this effortful behaviour into a sequence in the brain that creates habitual behaviour.

Use rewards

Learning new behaviour is linked to our brain reward system. When behaviour in a given context is rewarded, the behaviour and context are paired, and this association with reward makes it more likely to be repeated. How can we link reward to a desired behaviour so it is more likely to happen again? Well, many of our behaviours will be automatically rewarding: if I go outside at lunch, this will be rewarding in itself because I will enjoy it. Achievement is also rewarding, so just managing to go outside will give me a sense of reward, which means I'll want to do it again. You can boost this by tying in extra rewards, such as meeting a friend or getting a coffee when you go outside, for example. We also need to ensure a new habit doesn't become associated with negative feelings. This is why it's key to start small, because if we keep on achieving, we keep on feeling good, which pushes us to do it again. If we set ourselves up to fail, we feel bad and are more likely to give up before this behaviour becomes habitual.

Make it easy

The brain starts habits automatically in response to a cue, therefore breaking old habits is about reducing this automaticity and creating more friction (making it difficult to do it automatically). So, for my lunchtime habit, I can increase friction and reduce automaticity by putting my sandwich somewhere that's not easily accessible to me, so I can't just pick it up and eat it. This disrupts my brain's sequence of behaviours that form this habit. Conversely, creating a new habit is about increasing automaticity and reducing friction: making something as easy to do as possible, so you can do it with minimal effort. To reduce friction for my new habit of going outside, I might put my lunch in a rucksack and have my shoes on ready to go. Think about ways you can increase automaticity and reduce friction for new happiness habits, and the opposite for shifting old habits.

Actions for happiness

The output for our happiness is what we do in our daily lives. It's no use making a theoretical sandwich and then not acting on it. Ultimately, it's what we do day to day that impacts on how we feel and adds to our overall sense of wellbeing. Yet, as we've seen, so many things get in the way of creating the output for our happiness sandwich.

Let's think about this in terms of push and pull. We know certain things make us feel good yet we don't do them. We've got a yoga class booked, but once we're at home it seems overly effortful to push yourself off that sofa and go. Then there are the immediate rewards our brain pulls us towards. The tantalizing temptations that feel fantastic short term but leave us feeling not so good afterwards. We know they are false fillings in our happiness sandwich, but the draw of that reward is strong and pulls us in.

The brain is focused on future goals, and I'm sure nearly everyone has set a goal in their life. It might have been a New Year's resolution, or specific goals for achievements in work or life. Even if you've not deliberately set a goal, you will have worked towards things such as completing a task at work or gaining a qualification. Having meaningful goals is important for our happiness for a number of reasons. Firstly, they give us purpose and can create positive affect. They also have beneficial side effects, such as learning, a sense of reward, feeling part of something and social connection. How we build these goals is important too. How we view goals, set them and work towards them are essential components of our happiness sandwich output that can help build (or hinder) our happiness.

Everything I've talked about here also comes down to decisions. What decision will you make when you can't be bothered, or when you feel that short-term rewarding pull? The success of our happiness sandwich output is dependent on us making the decisions that help us live in a way that is conducive to wellbeing and happiness. Lots of things can hamper this decision-making, including habits, pushes and pulls. Let's return to the beginning (or Chapter 1, at least) to brain and happiness myths, because these are essential for decision-making. Our beliefs about happiness will influence our decisions. The brain's poor predictive abilities mean that often we predict things will make us feel happy when in fact they will do nothing of the sort, so we end up making decisions that are incompatible with happiness.

These exercises look at how we can increase push (and pull) when we want to, reduce the pull of false fillings and make decisions compatible with building happiness.

Planning for happiness (proactively creating the positive push and pull)

This is a simple exercise; however, its simplicity is also its strength. If we pre-plan something, we are far more likely to do it. So, look at what your happiness fillings are and plan them in. Schedule downtime into your diary. Plan your happiness fillings as an essential component of your life, not as an afterthought (because, after all, they are the point of life). To make your plans even less effortful, try getting everything ready beforehand (reducing friction and increasing automaticity). Make it as easy as possible for your brain to do the thing that will make you happy. So, if you have planned yoga, leave your mat/gym stuff at the door or in the car, so that having to find it won't become the friction that makes you not bother. Another simple way to make sure you carry out your plans is to use your 'second self', as Aristotle described it. Put simply, a second self is a friend, family member or work colleague. Scheduling something with someone else gives us a greater push and pull towards activities we want to do, makes us less likely to cancel, and often provides the cue to introduce a new habit. For example, I'm much more likely to go for my walk at lunchtime if I ask a friend to call for me. Here are some key points to consider for planning your happiness:

• *The happiness fillers I want to add are...*

• *How can I plan these in? How can I increase automaticity and reduce friction when planning? Can I use a second self to help with my planning?*

Beware immediate rewards

Let's go back to those false fillers you identified, or the false taps for your stress bucket (see page 129). How many of these are you pulled into by immediate reward, when you know you get a hit straight away that feels great but longer term not so much? Online shopping, social media likes, fast food and many other things all create an immediate reward hit for the brain. None of these things is inherently bad, but you need to recognize when the immediate reward is becoming too much of a pull and impacting negatively overall on your happiness. It might make you feel bad afterwards, it might not make you as happy as you hoped (a pile of new clothes building up might create stress, for example) or it may be sucking time away from things that would make you happy.

So, what can we do about these negative impacts? Create as much friction as possible so they are not automatic. Think about how you could do this for the false fillers you've identified. Put your phone away, remove card details from online sites, don't go into the context where these things happen. When you're not drawn in automatically, you have a chance to question your brain reward system's decision to pull you in. Use the prompts below to help:

• *My immediate rewards I need to be aware of are...*

• *How can I create friction around them?*

• *When I notice I am being pulled in, stop and think: will this help or hinder my happiness? You can also use the next exercise to help you decide what to do!*

Five elements for making happiness-compatible decisions

Let's put happiness at the centre of our decision-making. When faced with a choice, consider these five elements:

1. Contributing factors to your happiness, i.e. your happiness fillers. Think about the factors that contribute towards your happiness in your life. Which choice best aligns with this?

2. Other factors that may drive your decision. Are you being influenced by any false beliefs, which are pushing you to make decisions unaligned with happiness? Identify these false beliefs and remind yourself of your happiness facts and your new metrics of success (see page 97). Which choice fits best with these?

3. Are you making false predictions about what will make you happy? Think back to similar decisions you have made, or consult other people, who will help keep those brain biases in check.

4. Balance meaning with stress. Sometimes it isn't just about choosing the joyful things, it's also about doing things – possibly tough things – that bring you meaning. However, take care that this doesn't create too much stress, which can become unhelpful.

5. Don't sweat the small stuff. When it comes to inconsequential stuff, like which shoes to wear, research says that you shouldn't deliberate too long. Instead, apply a principle called 'satisficing' – go for a 'good enough' option. The small things have negligible impact on your happiness.

Designing your context for happiness

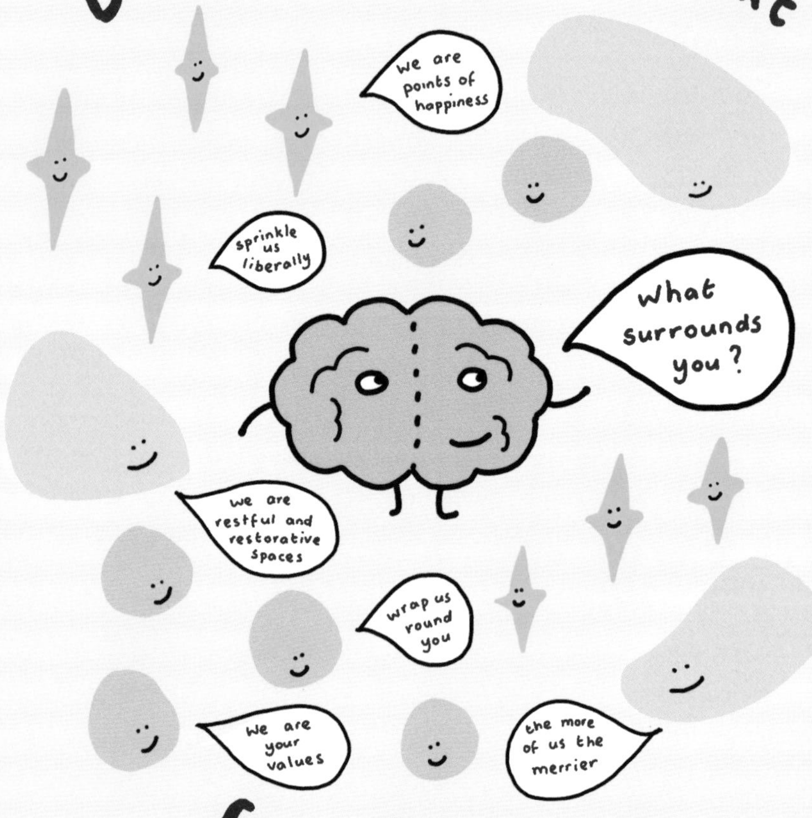

Designing your context for happiness

I see many a meme stating 'Happiness comes from within' and yes, how we perceive and interact with the world are important factors for happiness. But everything exists in a context, and this is a crucial component of everybody's happiness sandwich. I still remember the beautiful plant I had in my flat as a student – although I tended carefully to it, it was never happy. The problem was, no matter what I did it was never going to be happy – this plant longed for tropical climes, which my draughty Scottish flat was never going to provide. I could have blamed the plant or myself, but realistically it needed a different context to make it happy.

Context is equally as important for humans. How we perceive our world is important, but if we start seeing this as everything, we start to place the blame of unhappiness and full responsibility for happiness on the individual. This is problematic. Yes we want to increase resilience, so that we can deal with stressful situations, but we also need to look at changing the context when it is detrimental. This is relevant in both personal and work situations. Telling somebody they need to cope better when their work load is unmanageable is unhelpful. The same applies in your personal life. Telling someone who faces daily bullying, for example, that they need to cope with it better to be happy is not only patronizing, but also suggests they are somehow to blame for the complex systemic and cultural factors that create stress, difficult emotions and negate happiness. It places the responsibility back on the individual, thereby creating even more stress.

There's lots of research to show how context is important to happiness: people who have access to green spaces have higher happiness levels; people who work in organizations with a safe and supportive culture feel and work better; people who experience discrimination or bullying have higher levels of unhappiness. If our context makes us feel safe and valued, we are less stressed and happier.

Of course, not all aspects of context can be changed easily. You may be trapped in a difficult work situation because you need money to pay your mortgage. In such situations it's important to separate context from self. Bear in mind that the context is crucial for how you are feeling, seek support, talk things through and problem-solve, if possible.

It is also important to think about the aspects of context that are in your control. Which elements get in the way of building your sandwich, distract you from it or create barriers to using it? Which elements make it easier for you to build your sandwich and support you in doing so?

Creating restful and restorative spaces

Places and spaces can provoke particular feelings, and some are conducive to happiness. Think of a space where you felt comfortable, where you felt your body relax. What was it about this space that made you feel that way? Were there particular physical aspects of the space that were comforting? Were there items in the space that made you feel happy? When you step into comforting spaces it helps engage your body's rest and digest system, and mitigates stress.

What exists in your environment can also be important for happiness. A study with women found that those who described their living spaces as 'restful and restorative' as opposed to 'cluttered' were less likely to be depressed or fatigued. Having a cluttered environment may make focusing on particular tasks more difficult, as there are more distractions and it can make it harder for us to attend to what we need to. So, if your space makes you feel shameful, sad, anxious or generally bad, it may be worth considering some small steps you can take to change this. Start, for example, by creating one or two restful and restorative spaces and building from there.

Follow this summary of key points to get started:

• *What are the aspects of my space that impact negatively on my happiness? How can I tackle these?*

• *What are the aspects of my space that make me feel happy, relaxed or restored? How can I increase or expand these?*

Add points of happiness in your context

What you have in your environment can be important for happiness in several ways. While certain items can be distracting and use capacity, others can be relaxing, remind you of happy times or provide moments of joy. Plants in my environment bring me happiness, as I find them relaxing and enjoy taking time to look after them (but too many and they start to make me feel overwhelmed). Photos, too, can provide memories of good experiences and places. Think about how you can create points of happiness throughout your day. When adding any items to your environment, think about how they will contribute (or not) to happiness as you go about your everyday life.

- *Which points in my context make me feel good?*

- *Can I add any happiness points in my context?*

Surround yourself with values

Research shows that if we are surrounded with people with similar values to us, we feel better. I'm not suggesting we should be surrounded by automatons who all think the same, because thinking about and hearing different views can increase happiness. However, people can differ hugely in their views, personalities and beliefs yet have similar values. We can use this knowledge in two ways to help with our happiness.

1. Holding on to guiding values can help people with differing viewpoints work together, because they know they are working to similar principles or towards shared goals. Remembering shared values when we are frustrated and annoyed at other people's stance can help us tolerate their viewpoint.

2. Thinking of the values of those around us can help us make decisions about where and with whom we want to spend our time, to make us happiest. Many moons ago I was in the fortunate position of having to choose between two jobs – one was the job I thought I'd always wanted, the other a curveball. I chose the curveball because when I met the people I would be working with, I knew they aligned with my values and felt I could work better and feel happier surrounded by them. I doubted myself for ages and worried I'd regret it, but looking back it was a great decision because it allowed me to be surrounded by my values. Feeling recognized and psychologically safe is more important for your job satisfaction than the specific content of what you do.

So, think about what values are important to you in people:

What values in those around you make you feel safe, secure and happy? Try thinking about someone you value or you admire to help with this.

When you are making decisions about who to spend time with (for example, work colleagues or friends), what shared values are important to you? Which people around you energize and support you and which sap your energy and make you feel bad? Use this knowledge to help decide how to spend your time and with whom.

Chapter 6
When Happiness Goes Astray

No matter who you are, or how much knowledge you have about what makes a decent happy sandwich or how rigorously you apply this, none of us are immune to life. Every single one of us will at times encounter sadness and suffering, and even with the most robust base and well-constructed sandwich, this will impact on us. It would be strange if it didn't. It is normal to feel difficult emotions when difficult events occur. The brain is identifying a tough time and reacting accordingly, as it should. Suffering and experiencing difficult emotions are, sadly, a normal part of life. Sometimes this will impact on us to the extent that happiness seems to elude us. At some point during our lives, we might also find our mental health is suffering, as many, many people do. Happiness is not just about how we increase our wellbeing, it's equally about how we learn to deal with and respond to suffering. This chapter looks at how to look after ourselves when times are bad, when we feel anything but happy, and when our mental health and wellbeing is poor.

Why am I finding this so Difficult?

Is it because ......

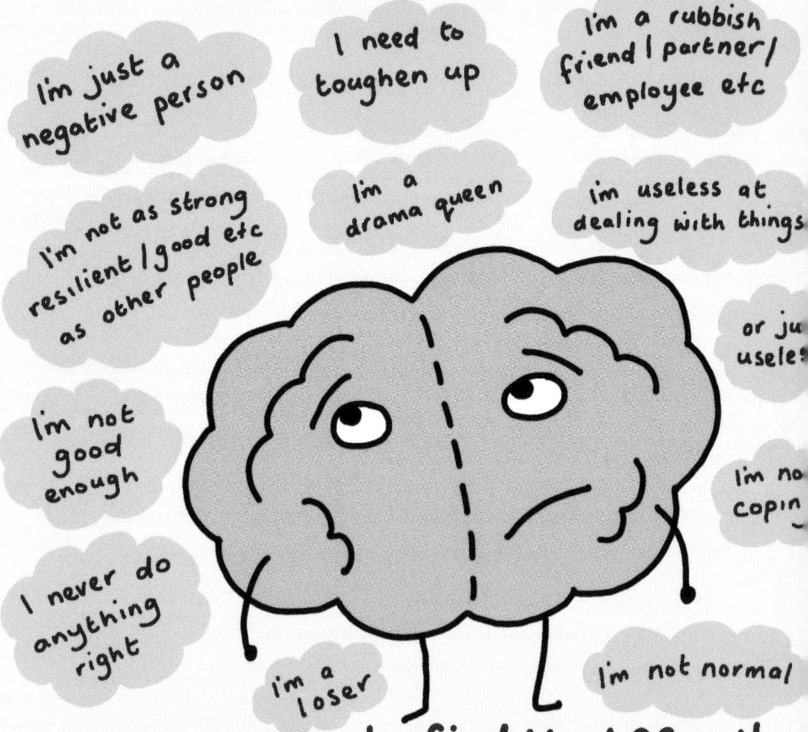

... or maybe I find it difficult because it is difficult and struggling is part of life

When life extracts happiness

As suffering is a normal part of life, we have to learn how to live life to increase happiness while also responding to suffering. If we think about it, sadness and other difficult emotions are a requirement for happiness. The contrast with sadness enables us to experience and recognize happiness, and may also help us truly appreciate happiness. Of course, these words of wisdom didn't stem from my brain, they have been the thought processes of people trying to make sense of life for many thousands of years. Nearly every religion talks about suffering as part of life and tries to explain it. Ancient philosophers thought understanding sadness was a requirement for wellbeing. In modern times, many of us don't experience day-to-day suffering; therefore, we can be surprised when it happens. However, it remains and always will be an integral, but difficult, component of life.

If we work towards happiness with the idea that it will make us immune to suffering, then our expectations (and most likely our happiness) will be dashed. When we experience difficult life events, we are likely to experience an array of challenging emotions alongside them, no matter who we are and how happy, resilient or able to cope we consider ourselves to be. It's a myth that coping is never experiencing these difficulties with emotion and remaining always happy. As a psychologist, I consider coping to be knowing what to do when you experience difficult emotions, and responding in a way that will help you return to happiness in the longer term.

However, as humans, when we feel distressed, our brain often finds it hard to take the course of action it knows will help, and we may follow paths that seem less effortful yet can extend our suffering. Changes in the brain when stressed mean we are less likely to be able to step back and look at a situation as we normally would and take the action we might normally take. At times of suffering and distress, the natural patterns the brain falls into can make it work against us.

While you may not be able to stop suffering, you can think about how you respond. Years of research have identified what helps people when they live through difficult times, despite sometimes experiencing vast and unimaginable life stressors that should have floored them. That's not to say their experiences didn't floor them at some point, because that's normal, yet they are able to live through huge adversity and experience happiness again, when we might have expected a more negative outcome. From this, we can learn what can help when we experience suffering in our own lives.

The next few exercises are based on the research around the factors that help people get through difficult life events, as well as on personal stories from the many amazing people I have met through my work.

'Why not me?' – accepting suffering as part of life

Suffering is inevitable, yet when it happens many people ask, 'Why me?' This can be a fruitless search that makes suffering seem unfair, discriminatory and focuses attention on finding a reason or sometimes allocating blame (frequently directed at ourselves) when often there is none. Another way to look at the situation is to ask, 'Why *not* me?' I first heard this in a TED talk by resilience researcher Dr Lucy Hone when talking about how she responded to her own traumatic events (see Further Reading, pages 188-9). This is not about accepting that bad things can never be changed and not having difficult emotions or getting angry, rather it's recognizing that this is part of life and focusing our actions and thoughts in a way that is beneficial to us.

In his book *The Art of Happiness* (yes, the one I read next to that rusty lamppost in Glasgow), the Dalai Lama talks about seeing suffering as something that is a natural part of existence, which lessens your sense of being a victim and makes you more tolerant towards suffering. No one is pretending you will ever enjoy feeling bad, but seeing it as a part of life seems to help people move through suffering to the other side. Refer back to the illustration on page 105 to remind yourself to recognize the common humanity of experiences.

Finding meaning in adversity

This concept sometimes does not go down well, so bear with me. As humans, finding meaning in our dark times appears to help us. Psychologists use a term called 'positive adjustment', which captures that people often feel they have been changed for the better having come through tough times. People tell me they have become a more empathetic person after adversity, that they wouldn't change the awful thing that happened because now they are grateful for the small things, appreciate their time and are happier as a result. This might sound like a cheesy Hollywood film, but hearing it from people who have been through a tough time is incredibly powerful. However, in the midst of a tough time, when we are feeling our worst, this idea can seem like a ridiculous notion. Yet, it's worth bearing in mind that what seems like the worst possible scenario can sometimes bring great meaning, and may even change your life in a strangely positive way. I'm not going to pretend any of us want to suffer, but people usually cope better than they think they will, and can come out the other side feeling they have developed in some way, which has a positive effect on their life going forward.

This exercise is NOT about putting a positive slant on your difficult experiences or emotions. We need to recognize and validate how tough situations can be. Please note this exercise may not be helpful in the immediate aftermath of difficult events or for certain events, so do not attempt this if it feels distressing and only do this if it feels right for you.

Some prompts to help find meaning at tough times:

Have I learned anything through this that will help in my life going forward?

Were there any unexpected positive outcomes from this difficult time (for example, it opened up possibilities, shifted life down an unexpected path to other experiences)?

Can I use my experience and knowledge to benefit others?

Is there anything new I can create or do as result of this that is meaningful to me?

Do I look at and respond to the world differently as a result of my experiences? Has this been helpful in any way?

Is there anything I can take from this experience about what really matters to me? How can I use this going forward?

What can I understand from my experience about how I want to live my life going forward?

Holding on to hope

Remember, the brain relies on how it feels currently to predict the future. This is great if we are feeling good, but if we are feeling bad, it's difficult to see a future that feels anything other than rubbish. This can add to a sense of hopelessness that makes us feel even worse. To find a way around the brain's design flaw, you need to remind it (and yourself) that the way you are feeling now is not a constant. You can direct your brain's attention to signs of hope and remind it to hold on to these to predict a different future.

What hope means will be entirely personal to you and your circumstances. It could be as simple as reminding yourself you won't always feel this way, or thinking over how you got through tough times before. This could be through looking at photos of good times, speaking to someone else about it or hearing words that are meaningful to you. It could be noticing small things that make you feel good – the spring flowers blooming or the laughter of your child. A powerful way to do this is hearing other people's stories of positive change that they never thought would happen. Matt Haig and Jonny Benjamin often use their own experiences of how they felt at their worst, to remind people to hold on to hope when they are at their lowest (see Further Reading, pages 188-9). This is hard for a distressed brain to do but is really important. Use the image opposite to identify the signs of hope that you can hold on to in your particular situation.

The Mental Health Hill:
being aware of and proactively caring for your mental health

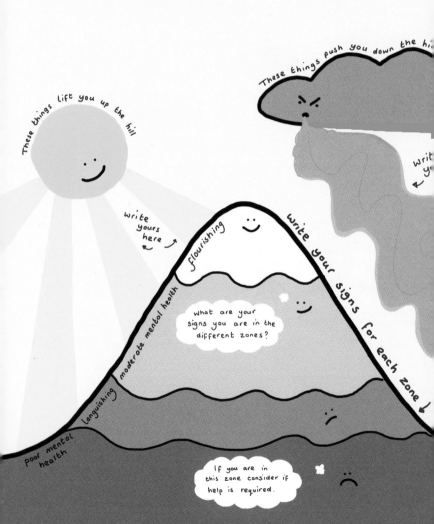

These things lift you up the hill

These things push you down the hill

write yours here →

write you ←

flourishing

moderate mental health

languishing

poor mental health

write your signs for each zone

what are your signs you are in the different zones?

If you are in this zone consider if help is required.

When happiness eludes you

Let's return to the wellbeing curve in the introduction (see page 6). Remember the categories? They don't represent different groups of people, rather different people at different times, because we can change category throughout life. We may find ourselves flourishing at one point, but then fall into the languishing or poor mental health category at another. So far, this book has looked at boosts to happiness and how we can add these to our daily lives and push ourselves up the wellbeing curve. Yet, to fully understand our wellbeing and act to improve it, we need to consider the full curve. We can't neglect those bits at the bottom as if they don't apply to us, because they apply to everybody.

Before you flick past this section thinking it's irrelevant to you, let me tell you why it is anything but. We often think experiencing poor mental health is something unusual, maybe even abnormal. If we look at the bottom category of poor mental health, a statistic may come into your mind, which says that one in four people will experience mental health difficulties. One in four of us already seems a lot, but let's dig down deeper. Studies often underestimate the amount of people who experience poor mental health for lots of reasons, including people not quite meeting the criteria for diagnosis despite feeling bad and under-reporting due to feelings of shame and stigma.

Longer-term studies, which look across a person's lifespan, suggest this number is likely to be much higher, at 60 per cent or above. Studies from the Dunedin Group in New Zealand suggest that this may be higher still and that around 80 per cent of us, possibly more, will experience mental health difficulties at some point. That's an awful lot of people. It seems poor mental health may not be abnormal at all. Perhaps we need to say that it is a common and shared experience that many people will have in the course of their life.

Now let's think about 'languishing' – the next category in the curve. In an article in *The New York Times*, psychologist Adam Grant described languishing as 'the void between depression and flourishing – the absence of wellbeing'. I wonder if you will be able to find *anyone* who, in the course of their lifetime, has not fallen into the languishing category. I very much doubt it, which is why this article resonated with so many people and was shared by millions around the world.

Ultimately, we need to consider distress as a normal part of life, because life can be tough and stressful for most of us at some point. Of course, it's way beyond the scope of this book to give advice on treating mental ill health, because it is complex. There is a range of types of difficulties you may experience, and the causes, contributors, triggers and symptoms can be as individual and different to each and every person as their own fingerprint. This means that treatments need to be individualized and what works for one person will be unique to them.

However, what this book can do, firstly, is help you understand your own mental health, so you can identify when it starts to go wrong and take pre-emptive action when required. Another crucial part of understanding your wellbeing is knowing when you need additional help. In general terms, if you have been experiencing difficult emotions that are impacting on your day-to-day life and/or functioning for more than two weeks, then it's worth considering if additional help may be beneficial. There is now a range of treatments, including psychological and therapeutic approaches, medicine and social/exercise prescriptions. Knowing the type of help there is and how to access it proactively is extremely powerful information to have at your fingertips, and learning this when you are feeling okay means you don't have to make an already depleted brain work hard to find this information when it is feeling bad and doesn't feel able to.

Secondly, while it may not always be possible to pinpoint an exact cause for mental health difficulties, we can say for a fact that your mental illness is not caused by some inherent flaw or something you have done wrong. It is something we all experience to some degree.

Thirdly, a distressed or depressed brain is not your friend, and probably not even your frenemy. I always think that it's a brain design flaw that at times of poor mental health, stress or overload, the brain seems to do the opposite of what we need it to do. Our negative ninja goes into hyperdrive mode, spotting every single negative, even when there is none. Our brain's fairly sensible managers and executives get the sack and we find it difficult to untangle what's going on, problem-solve ways out, manage our attention or even to stand back from our thoughts and see them with perspective. Even the basics like sleep and appetite go out the window. Knowing this doesn't mean it won't happen, because the design flaw is inherent to all our brains, but it does mean you can spot it. This gives you an advantage because you can work around it, instead of just going with it.

Lastly, distressed brains don't need more complexity thrown at them, they're feeling overwhelmed enough without adding more. Even the most basic of decisions can feel overwhelming when you're feeling bad (remember, your brain has given its executives the sack), so sometimes the best strategies are the simplest.

Here, we'll look at some simple strategies that even the most overwhelmed brain can use when it's feeling rubbish (but which can also be used at other times).

Your mental health hill

Use the illustration on page 174 to help you notice signs for different stages of the wellbeing curve. What are the signs you are flourishing? What are the signs you are languishing? Now, this might be a learning process over time, but you can start to get to know yourself and recognize the signs for the different zones. The sun and the wind represent the things that push you up the hill (are positive for your wellbeing) and down the hill (impact negatively). Understanding these can help you act when you notice your mental health and wellbeing deteriorating and know when to seek help. You can also separate your signs into thinking, emotional, physical and behavioural categories, as we did with the stress bucket (see page 128).

Self-stigmatizing ourselves

How often do you feel bad and then start to stigmatize yourself? This can be saying you shouldn't be feeling the way you are, your inner critic having free reign, or calling yourself all manner of horrible words for how you feel: pathetic, weak, abnormal. At these times, compassion can seem too complicated and rationalizing your thoughts impossible, so simple reminders are best. This could be having short statements, exercises or prompts to hand to remind you this is not the case. You could screenshot something on your phone, or keep a page of nice messages you

This is your pilot light

(inspired by Bryony Gordon)

 will
what
you
do

stoke
it up?

Blow
it
out?

or

have received or direct links to things you find helpful. Again, I would recommend Tara Brach's RAIN Meditation, which serves as a prompt and reminder that suffering is normal and encourages kindness and understanding for yourself (see Further Reading, pages 188-9). As a reminder of the normality of feeling bad, I also love Bryony Gordon's words: 'I used to think that the way I felt made me a freak, that it made me somehow not normal. Now I know it's the most normal thing to feel this way.'

EXERCISE 3

Will this help or hinder?

When we are feeling bad, our brain is often pulled automatically towards things that don't help us and gets caught in patterns that make us feel worse. An extremely simple task is to ask yourself when you plan to do something: Does this help or hinder me? Try to increase those that help and decrease those that hinder.

Bryony Gordon's analogy of a pilot light captured this perfectly for me. Using the illustration opposite, imagine you are the pilot light of a decrepit boiler. When you do something, ask yourself, is this going to stoke my boiler light and keep it alight, or is it going to blow it out? Choose the action that stokes your boiler light and stay away from the things that try to blow it out. While this is a simple and undemanding task that can be used even when your brain is feeling bad, you could also use it throughout your life to help with your happiness and wellbeing when making decisions.

Happiness, more or less

So, there you have it: happiness, more or less. But hopefully, more of it now that you've worked your way through to the conclusion of this book. We've busted some myths about happiness, thought about what happiness really is, built up the components of your happiness sandwich from the base upwards, and thought about how to input and output from your sandwich effectively, by using your attention and building happiness actions into your life. Now that you've come to the end of the book, you can question those false beliefs about what makes us happy and about happiness itself. You can see happiness as something that each and every one of us can build into our life. You can identify the looming threats to your happiness sandwich and act to guard against them. You can spot when that pesky brain of yours is working against you and your wellbeing. Most importantly, even if I've not managed to convince you that happiness is the point of life, you can at least see it as something that is worth building towards, and you can take action to do this, as an integral part of your life.

However, I'm afraid to say that you haven't earned a free pass to Happyland, where you're welcomed with a never-ending smile into the land of eternal joy (because we know it doesn't exist). Happiness, like anything worthwhile, requires work, and that work continues throughout life as we learn what helps us, what truly brings us happiness and how we can take effective action for happiness in day-to-day life. Happiness is inherently transient, so that work is as much about learning to appreciate and grow the pockets of happiness as it is manoeuvring our way through the inevitable difficulties we face. The evidence points to that work being worthwhile, and we can use this knowledge to construct our lives in a way that is orientated towards happiness.

As for me, I have navigated a tough time, as many of us have during the Covid-19 pandemic, to return to the things that make me feel good and bring meaning to my life. These are not monumental milestones but small daily actions: connecting with people I love; sharing fun moments with friends; watching my seeds grow; taking time to relax; reading a book; getting out and enjoying the Scottish scenery; beating my husband at badminton; connecting with people towards a shared purpose at work, and finding meaning in these moments along the way. Yet, like all of us, these attempts to add happiness fillers into my life have sometimes gone amiss. As I write this, I have my arm in a sling as a fun game of Twister (a bribed attempt to connect with my children) led to a trip to A&E. This was not so much a false filling but a happiness filling that slid off the sandwich and landed heavily on my arm. We all get it wrong, insert the wrong fillings or have our sandwich collapse unexpectedly, but we can learn to navigate through and build it back up again with what we've learned. That's what happiness needs from us: holding on to hope through tough times and building up again.

Of course, it would be remiss not to highlight the obvious fact that I have predominantly focused on what we can do as individuals to manage and increase our own happiness. I've mentioned connections and interactions with those around us as these are crucial for happiness. However, building happiness goes beyond individuals; we need to consider it in context. That context may be your workplace, your household, your community, your neighbourhood, your country or even your government. Wellbeing and happiness are (and need to be) everyone's business, because they are as much about how we build the context to enable them as how we build our lives.

Let's start with work. To be happy at work, we need a culture that makes us feel safe and valued. Workplaces need to develop that culture and create a psychologically safe space that has wellbeing at the heart of it. This requires collective effort from those within an organization, supported by leaders from the top. Just as it's worth the effort for individuals to work towards happiness, it's also worth the effort for workplaces to put wellbeing at the heart of their organization. Workplaces with happier employees have increased innovation, reduced staff turnover, less staff sickness, greater engagement and collective effort from staff and, in financial terms, they also have reduced costs and tend to perform better.

What about communities? Community wellbeing is about creating the context for communities to flourish, as well as the individuals within them. It's about building places that enable people to access nature and community spaces, and provide safe and secure houses. It's about providing the places that allow people to engage in wellbeing activities, including exercise, social interaction, fresh air and nature. It's about providing community-integrated support proactively and, at times when we know people are vulnerable, to reduce isolation and improve health and wellbeing. It's about people feeling safe and secure in their life and community. (If you think these ideas seem lofty, just wait until the next paragraph!)

As for government, well, I agree with the words of the organization What Works Wellbeing, which says that the aim of all government policies should be to improve lives – and we cannot evaluate a policy without considering its impact on wellbeing. Wellbeing is more than mental health policies. It's about providing safe and affordable housing, providing support to the vulnerable and for those who are suffering, access to healthcare, reducing systemic inequalities, tackling poverty and discrimination, and ensuring children have the best start in life. Overall, it's about offering hope, providing support when needed, reducing suffering, and creating the opportunities and context that allow people to engage with what makes them happy and well. Surely the point of government is to help people live well, and that is not just about one aspect of life, it covers all aspects of life. While some countries have started to measure national happiness alongside GDP, perhaps we need to go further and measure the wellbeing impact of all policies and consider wellbeing and happiness as central indicators of success.

So, the responsibility for wellbeing and happiness does not sit only with individuals, it is held collectively by communities, workplaces, organizations and government. While you may want to improve happiness at these levels, because that's likely to be very meaningful and increase your own happiness, you need to start with what you can control and build happiness on a daily basis. It's back to those circles of control again, and that means looking at what you can do in your life, and for those around you, to put happiness at the core.

Start building your happiness sandwich today – in fact, start now. Which happiness fillers can you do today that make you feel good and give you meaning? Build on this to ensure that you are putting your happiness and wellbeing at the heart of your life, through what you do, how you respond to hard times, how you treat others, the decisions you make and the actions you take. It's not an afterthought – it's what makes this life worthwhile on a daily basis and it adds up over the course of a lifetime. Happiness, after all, is the purpose of life. On that note, because we know acts of kindness help happiness, I'm off to drive to Glasgow with a book, to find that rusty lamppost…

Further Reading

You can find out more about some of the topics discussed in this book with these further resources.

Hepburn, Emma, *A Toolkit for Modern Life*, Greenfinch, 2020

Introduction

His Holiness The Dalai Lama and Cutler, Howard C., *The Art of Happiness: A Handbook for Living*, Hodder & Stoughton, 1999

What Works Wellbeing – wellbeing definition: https://whatworkswellbeing.org/about-wellbeing/what-is-wellbeing/

More on the history of happiness/wellbeing: https://www.pursuit-of-happiness.org/history-of-happiness/

More on the wellbeing curve/continuum: Huppert, F.A., 'Psychological Well-Being: Evidence Regarding Its Causes and Consequences', *Applied Psychology: Health and Well-Being*, 1: 137–164, 2009

Chapter 1: Understanding Happiness

Gilbert, Dan, *Stumbling on Happiness*, Harper Perennial, 2007

Dr Laurie Santos' podcast, The Happiness Lab, in discussion with Dr Dan Gilbert: https://www.happinesslab.fm/season-1-episodes/the-unhappy-millionaire

Baumeister, Roy F. et al, 'Bad is Stronger than Good', *Review of General Psychology*, 5, 323–370, 2001

Burnett, Dean, *The Happy Brain: The Science of Where Happiness Comes From, and Why*, Guardian Faber Publishing, 2019

Lyubomirsky, Sonja, 'Hedonic Adaptation to Negative and Positive Experiences', in Folkman, Susan (ed.), *The Oxford Handbook of Stress, Health, and Coping*, OUP, 2010

Lyubomirsky, Sonja, *The Myths of Happiness*, Penguin Group, 2014

Chapter 2: What Makes Us Happy?

For more on happiness and connections: The Harvard Study of Adult Development study: https://www.adultdevelopmentstudy.org

Acts of kindness ideas: https://www.actionforhappiness.org https://www.randomactsofkindness.org/kindness-ideas

A guide to understanding your values: https://www.worldvaluesday.com/wp-content/uploads/2021/05/WVD-2021-Values-Guide-for-Individuals.pdf

A range of tools to help identify your values by Russ Harris: https://www.actmindfully.com.au

A specific values exercise to try: https://www.actmindfully.com.au/wp-content/uploads/2019/07/Values_Checklist_-_Russ_Harris.pdf

The science of awe: https://ggsc.berkeley.edu/images/uploads/GGSC-JTF_White_Paper-Awe_FINAL.pdf

Awe practises: https://ggia.berkeley.edu/#filters=awe

Frankl, Viktor, *Man's Search for Meaning*, Rider Books, 2021

Tribole, Evelyn & Resch, Elyse, *Intuitive Eating: A Revolutionary Anti-Diet Approach*, St Martin's Essentials, 2020

Chapter 3: Perceiving Happiness

Tara Brach's RAIN meditation: https://tarabrach.ac-page.com/rain-pdf-download

Kirschner, H., Kuyken, W., Wright, K., Roberts, H., Brejcha, C., & Karl, A., 'Soothing Your Heart and Feeling Connected: A New Experimental Paradigm to Study the Benefits of Self-Compassion', *Clinical Psychological Science*, 7(3), 545–565, 2019

Dr Kristin Neff's website with practical exercises for increasing self-compassion: https://self-compassion.org

Dr Kristin Neff's TED talk, 'The Space Between Self-Esteem and Self-Compassion'

Nickerson, Raymond, 'Confirmation Bias: A Ubiquitous Phenomenon in Many Guises', *Review of General Psychology*, 1998

Rosing, Hans, *Factfulness: Ten Reasons We're Wrong About the World – and Why Things Are Better Than You Think*, Sceptre, 2018

Williams, Mark and Penman, Danny, Mindfulness: A Practical Guide to Finding Peace in a Frantic World, Piatkus Books, 2011

Nudge your attention towards the good:
https://thehappynewspaper.com
https://www.upworthy.com
https://www.goodnewsnetwork.org/

Chapter 4: Protecting Happiness
Dwyer, R., Kushlev, K., & Dunn, E., 'Smartphone Use Undermines Enjoyment of Face-to-Face Social Interactions', *Journal of Experimental Social Psychology*, 78, 233–239, 2018

Dr Laurie Santos' podcast, The Happiness Lab, in discussion with Catherine Price:
https://www.happinesslab.fm/season-2-episodes/episode-6-dial-d-for-distracted

Hammond, Claudia, The Art of Rest: How to Find Respite in the Modern Age, Canongate, 2019

Chapter 5: Building Happiness
Clear, James, Atomic Habits: An Easy & Proven Way to Build Good Habits & Break Bad Ones, Cornerstone, 2018

Behaviour scientist, B.J. Fogg's Tiny Habits website, https://www.tinyhabits.com/start-tiny

Chapter 6: When Happiness Goes Wrong
Benjamin, Jonny, *The Stranger on the Bridge: My Journey from Suicidal Despair to Hope*, Bluebird, 2019

Benjamin, Jonny, *The Book of Hope: 101 Voices on Overcoming Adversity* Hardcover, Bluebird, 2021

Caspi A., Houts R.M., Ambler A., et al., 'Longitudinal Assessment of Mental Health Disorders and Comorbidities Across 4 Decades Among Participants in the Dunedin Birth Cohort Study', JAMA Netw Open. 2020

Gordon, Bryony, *No Such Thing As Normal*, Headline, 2021

Adam Grant's *New York Times* article on languishing:
https://www.nytimes.com/2021/04/19/well/mind/covid-mental-health-languishing.html

Haig, Matt, *Reasons to Stay Alive*, Canongate, 2015

Dr Lucy Hone's TED talk, 'The Three Secrets of Resilient People', https://www.ted.com/talks/lucy_hone_the_three_secrets_of_resilient_people

Conclusion – Happiness, more or less:
Hardoon, Deborah, 'Wellbeing Evidence at the Heart of Policy', What Works Wellbeing, https://whatworkswellbeing.org/wp-content/uploads/2020/02/WEHP-full-report-Feb2020_.pdf

Acknowledgements
A book is never just built by one person. This book was brought to you by…

Those who carefully constructed it: my co-creator Julia (who has patiently run a marathon alongside me), Kerry, Katie, Ginny and my sh…sense checker, Jenny.

Those who can shout about it better than me: Ella and Lipfon, and the Greenfinch and Quercus teams.

Those who provided a secure base of time, support, laughs and infinite cups of tea: Stuart, Fraser and Evie (we'll never forget that game of twister now).

My many cheerleader chutneys: Susan, Rona, dual-role Jenny, Neil and all those that send random texts, nice cards and kind messages, despite me going MIA.

Last, but by no means least, my number one book fans, Sophie and Ruby, and my Inverurie and Falkirk PR teams.

Thank you to everyone who helped me build this book.

CHEERLEADER CHUTNEY

Index

First published in Great Britain in 2021 by

Greenfinch
An imprint of Quercus Editions Ltd
Carmelite House
50 Victoria Embankment
London EC4Y 0DZ

An Hachette UK company

A CIP catalogue record for this book is available from the British Library

HB ISBN 978-1-52941-618-3
ebook ISBN 978-1-52941-620-6
Digital audiobook ISBN 978-1-52941-619-0

10 9 8 7 6 5 4 3 2 1

Design by Ginny Zeal
Illustrations by Emma Hepburn
Cover design by Tokiko Morishima

Printed and bound in Croatia by Denona